REDUCE ME TO LOVE

UNLOCKING THE SECRET TO LASTING JOY

by
Joyce Meyer

WARNER
Faith™

NEW YORK   BOSTON

CONTENTS

INTRODUCTION

Loving and being loved is what makes life worth living. Many people have had times in their lives when they felt they were unloved or that they had no one to love. If they dwell constantly on those kinds of thoughts, it can cause them to be extremely unhappy and depressed. Some have even committed suicide as a result of these negative emotions.

Love is the energy of life. It is what motivates people to get up each day and keep going.

Love gives life purpose and meaning. The world is looking for love, but they are really looking for God, because God is love.

People look for fulfillment in life in different ways that may seem good at first, but often leave them feeling frustrated, disappointed and empty. Only by walking in love (putting love into action by continually reaching out to others and making an effort to show them love through various acts of kindness) can they find the true fulfillment they are so desperately seeking.

If you are sincere about wanting to walk in love, I would like to share with you what I have learned about love over the past twelve years.

I am still learning, and know I always will be. But I am grateful to God for the revelation He has given me about love. It has truly changed my life, and I am convinced it will change your life too — *if* you are willing to say, "Lord, eliminate everything in my life that is holding me back, anything that is keeping me from walking in love and finding true fulfillment in my life." In other words, "Lord, reduce me to love (bring me to a state or condition of completely walking in love)[1]!"

1

THE GREATEST OF
THESE IS LOVE

But earnestly desire and zealously cultivate the great-
est and best gifts and graces (the higher gifts and the
choicest graces). And yet I will show you a still more
excellent way [one that is better by far and the highest
of them all – love].

—1 CORINTHIANS 12:31

Where does love fit into your list of priorities? Jesus said, *A*
new commandment I give to you, that you love one another; as I have
loved you . . .(John 13:34 NKJV). It seems to me that Jesus was saying
love is the main thing on which we should concentrate.

The apostle Paul stated that *. . . faith, hope, love abide . . . but the*
greatest of these is love (1 Corinthians 13:13).

Love should be number one on our spiritual priority list. We
should study love, pray about love and develop the fruit of love
(according to Galatians 5:22,23, one of the nine fruit of the Spirit

available to those in whom God's Holy Spirit lives) by practicing loving others.

God is love, so when we walk in His love we abide in Him. Because we walk in God's love by receiving and expressing it, we should not deceive ourselves into thinking we can love God while we hate other people. (See 1 John 4:20.)

Love is the greatest thing in the world. It is the best thing to commit our life to, to seek to excel in.

We seek many things in the course of our lifetime. We hope to find fulfillment in each one, but most of them fall short of the desired goal. When we put our time and energy into things that do not fulfill us, we feel frustrated.

It took me about forty-five years to realize that my priorities were mixed up and that I was not making love the main thing in my life. It was not my first priority. The commitment to learn how to walk in love has been the single best decision I have ever made as a Christian.

Love not only blesses others; it also blesses the one doing the loving. Concentrating on being a blessing to others has brought me joy. I find it exciting. It challenges me.

All of us must become students of love; we must pray that God will *reduce us to love.*

FAITH WORKS BY LOVE

> *For [if we are] in Christ Jesus, neither circumcision*
> *nor uncircumcision counts for anything, but only faith*

*activated and energized and expressed and working
through love.*

—GALATIANS 5:6

We are normally taught that faith is the pinnacle of Christian virtues. We study it, try to exercise it, preach sermons on it, write books about it and encourage one another in it all the time.

Faith is vital; without it we cannot please God. (Hebrews 11:6.) Faith is not the price that buys the blessings of God, but it is the hand that receives them. "By grace, through faith" is how the blessings of our Lord and Savior come to His children. (Ephesians 2:8 KJV.)

Faith is very important, and yet according to 1 Corinthians 13:2 if we have enough faith to move mountains and have not love, we are nothing.

Galatians 5:6 says faith works (is energized) by love. Knowing the love of God for us as individuals, and learning to allow His love to flow through us to others, is the power behind faith. How can we place faith in God unless we are assured He loves us? How can we ask God to help us, and have confidence He will do so, if we are mistreating others? Our personal love walk gives us confidence before God and enables us to receive from Him what we ask for in prayer. (1 John 3:18-23.)

Love is also a distinguishing characteristic of the disciples of Christ. (John 13:35.)

LET YOUR LIGHT SHINE

By this shall all [men] know that you are My disciples, if you love one another [if you keep on showing love among yourselves].

—JOHN 13:35

We need to show the world Jesus. We do that by walking in His love — the love of the Father that was first revealed and expressed in His Son Jesus and is now manifested in us: *Let your light so shine before men that they may see your moral excellence and your praise-worthy, noble, and good deeds and recognize and honor and praise and glorify your Father Who is in heaven* (Matthew 5:16).

Jesus Himself taught on love and walked in love. He said, "If you have seen Me, you have seen the Father." (John 14:9.) The world is looking for something real, something tangible. They are looking for love, and God is love. (1 John 4:8.)

Many people have gone to church looking for God and have been met with the rules and regulations of religion. After encountering some of the Christians who "talk the talk" but who did not "walk the walk," they left without encountering God. Instead of drawing them in, many people's experience with churches and Christians has driven them away.

The fields are . . . *white already to harvest,* (John 4:35 KJV), but the Lord needs laborers. (Luke 10:2 KJV.) He needs Christians who are committed to developing the character of Jesus Christ in their own lives. According to 2 Corinthians 5:20, you and I are Christ's ambassadors — His personal representatives. The Lord is making His appeal to the world through us.

As previously stated, Jesus said that it is by love that all men will know who His disciples are:

> *I give you a new commandment: that you should love one another. Just as I have loved you, so you too should love one another.*

By this shall all [men] know that you are My disci-
ples, if you love one another [if you keep on showing
love among yourselves].

—JOHN 13:34, 35

Love is the trademark (distinctive sign or characteristic)[1] of the Christian. Before we purchase something we like to check its quality. As we shop, we read labels or we look for certain trademarks (brand names) that have a reputation for being good. That is what people should be able to do with us as disciples of Christ. They should be able to identify us not only by our talk, but also by our walk.

I want people to think of me as someone who loves them. I want to make them thirsty (have a strong desire)[2] for God. I want to be a light in their dark places.

There was a time when I wanted to be known as a powerful minister, a person who was successful and popular. I finally came to realize that true power and success is love.

CHANGING YOUR FOCUS

And this I pray: that your love may abound yet more
and more and extend to its fullest development in
knowledge and all keen insight [that your love may
display itself in greater depth of acquaintance and
more comprehensive discernment],

So that you may surely learn to sense what is vital, and
approve and prize what is excellent and of real value. . . .

—PHILIPPIANS 1:9, 10

Do you need to readjust your priorities or change your focus?

In Philippians 1:9,10, Paul prayed that the church in Philippi would abound in love and that their love would display itself in a greater way. He prayed they would learn to choose what was excellent and of real value. In 1 Corinthians 12:31, he wrote that love is the more excellent way.

Paul was praying that these believers would focus on love. We cannot have powerful, victorious lives unless we love people.

Are you willing and ready to become a student of the love walk? If so, you need to know that it requires education and commitment.

We must have our minds renewed to what love really is. It is not a feeling we have; it is a decision we make — a decision to treat people the way Jesus would treat them.

When we make a true commitment to walk in love, it usually causes a huge shift in our lifestyle. Many of our ways — our thoughts, our conversation, our habits — have to change. For instance, we may be accustomed to spending all our extra money on ourselves only to discover that walking in love requires that we spend it on others.

Love is tangible; it is not just an emotional feeling, a spiritual thing that cannot be seen or touched. It is evident to everyone who comes in contact with it.

A love walk does not come easily or without personal sacrifice. Each time we choose to love someone, it will cost us something — time, money or effort. That's why we are told to count the cost before we make the commitment. (Luke 14:25-33.)

PURSUE AND SEEK LOVE

Eagerly pursue and seek to acquire [this] love [make it your aim, your great quest]. . . .
—1 CORINTHIANS 14:1

Developing a love walk like the one displayed in the life of Jesus is like digging for gold. True Christlike love is not found on the surface of life. It cannot just be seen and picked up. The Bible tells us that we must eagerly *pursue* and *seek* it. These are both strong words.

The word *pursue* means "to follow in an effort to capture or overtake."[3] The word *seek* means "to try to find or discover; search for."[4] *In other words, we need to go after love with all our might and act as if we cannot live without it!*

There are degrees of desire. We want many things, but there are only a few things in life we actually want so much that we are willing to sacrifice to have them.

If you and I want to learn about love, we will have to study it. We will have to read books about it, listen to teaching tapes on it, familiarize ourselves with everything Jesus and the apostles said about it.

If you want to know about love, try to find someone who operates in love and study that individual. Watch how he handles people and difficult or tense situations. Observe how he gives. Examine the fruit in his life.

All of us must not only learn about love but also seek, pursue and acquire it, because God's Word boldly tells us that without it we are absolutely nothing.

THE GREATEST OF THESE IS LOVE

If I [can] speak in the tongues of men and [even] of angels, but have not love (that reasoning, intentional, spiritual devotion such as is inspired by God's love for and in us), I am only a noisy gong or a clanging cymbal.

And if I have prophetic powers (the gift of interpreting the divine will and purpose), and understand all the secret truths and mysteries and possess all knowledge, and if I have [sufficient] faith so that I can remove mountains, but have not love (God's love in me) I am nothing (a useless nobody).

Even if I dole out all that I have [to the poor in providing] food, and if I surrender my body to be burned or in order that I may glory, but have not love (God's love in me), I gain nothing.

—1 CORINTHIANS 13:1-3

This is strong language, but hopefully it will wake us up!

There are many people who think they are really something because of what they have accomplished in life, but according to God's Word they are nothing unless love has been a priority in their life.

A little girl who loved Jesus wanted to express her love for Him, so she asked her mother about it. She said that since she knew that Jesus lived in her heart she was wondering if she wrote "I love you" on a piece of paper and ate it, would He see it.

Of course, the way Jesus sees how much we love Him is by how much we obey Him. He has commanded us to love one another; if we are not doing that, then we are not showing Him that we love Him.

We can sacrifice without love, we can give without proper motive, we can build ministries and forget all about love, but there is nothing greater we can take to the unchurched world than love. There is nothing more convincing than God's love reflected in our own character.

Love is the universal language; everyone understands it. Even though the people of a remote village in India or Africa may not understand the language of the missionary who is sent to them, they can understand kindness, warmth and a caring attitude.

Why did Paul single out love as the greatest thing in the world? Because *love never fails . . .* (1 Corinthians 13:8). Everything else may fail, but love will not.

Love can melt the hardest heart, it can heal the wounds of the broken heart and it can quiet the fears of the anxious heart.

Most of the things we devote our time and energy to are things that are currently passing away, things that will not last, things that are not eternal.

We strive to make money, build businesses, achieve great accomplishments, excel in sports, be popular, own buildings, cars, clothes, jewelry. We want to expand our minds and see the world, yet all of these things are temporal. Only love never comes to an end. An act of love goes on and endures forever.

I want to put my time and energy into something lasting, don't you?

In his book, *The Greatest Thing in the World*, Henry Drummond says that "to love abundantly is to live abundantly, and to love for ever is to live for ever."[5] In order to "love abundantly" and "love forever," you must learn to walk in love toward everyone. But to do that you must first receive God's love for you, because it is impossible to give to others something you do not have yourself.

2

YOU CAN'T GIVE AWAY
SOMETHING YOU DON'T HAVE

"We love Him, because He first loved us."

—1 JOHN 4:19

As soon as I made a commitment of my life to the Lord Jesus Christ, I began to hear sermons about the importance of loving others. I desired to walk in love, but it truly seemed I could not. I had the urge, but no power to perform it. (Romans 7:18.) I made elaborate plans, but always failed at carrying them out.

Unfulfilled desire is often frustrating. I felt very frustrated and wondered what was wrong with me. I was impatient with people, legalistic and harsh, judgmental, rude, selfish, unforgiving — and that is only the beginning of the list.

A breakthrough in understanding came when God began to show me that I could not love others because I had never received His love for me. I mentally acknowledged the Bible teaching that God loved me, but it was not a reality in my heart. I was like a thirsty person with a glass of water sitting in front of him who remained thirsty because he never drank the water.

Love has a beginning and a completion. First, God loves us, and by faith we receive His love. We then love ourselves in a balanced way, we give love back to God and we learn to love other people. Love must follow this course or it is not complete.

ARE YOU LOVABLE?

. . . God shows and clearly proves His [own] love for us by the fact that while we were still sinners, Christ (the Messiah, the Anointed One) died for us.

—ROMANS 5:8

As soon as you saw the heading on this section, "Are You Lovable?", you may have immediately thought, "No, I'm not!"

I would have probably responded the same way to that question before I came to understand the true nature of God's love and His reason for loving me.

How can God love us as imperfect as we are? He can because He *wants to;* it pleases Him: *For He foreordained us (destined us, planned in love for us) to be adopted (revealed) as His own children through Jesus Christ, in accordance with the purpose of His will [because it pleased Him and was His kind intent]* (Ephesians 1:5).

God loves because that is His nature. God *is* love. (1 John 4:8.) If He were otherwise, He would not be Who He is.

God always loves us! He may not always love everything we do, but He does love us. God's love is unconditional; it is based on Him, not us!

GOD'S GRACE IS GREATER THAN OUR SIN

But then Law came in, [only] to expand and increase the trespass [making it more apparent and exciting opposition]. But where sin increased and abounded, grace (God's unmerited favor) has surpassed it and increased the more and superabounded.

—ROMANS 5:20

God conquers evil with good. (Romans 12:21.) He does that by pouring out His limitless grace upon us so that if we sin, His grace becomes greater than our sin. Just as it is impossible for God not to love, so it is impossible for us to do anything to keep Him from loving us.

God's love is the power that forgives our sins, heals our emotional wounds and mends our broken hearts. (See Psalm 147:3.)

Once you realize that you are loved by God, not because of anything you are or anything you have done, then you can quit trying to deserve His love or earn His love and simply receive it and enjoy it.

Start by confessing that God loves you. Say it out loud several times a day when you are alone. Speak it out into the atmosphere and get used to hearing it — get comfortable with the thought of it. Bask in His love, soak in it and let it saturate your soul — your thinking and emotions. Imagine the glory of it, **"God loves me!"**

Once your heart is filled with the knowledge of God's love, you can begin to love Him in return: *We love Him, because He first loved us.*

KNOW THE LOVE OF GOD

May Christ through your faith [actually] dwell (settle down, abide, make His permanent home) in your hearts! May you be rooted deep in love and founded securely on love,

That you may have the power and be strong to apprehend and grasp with all the saints [God's devoted people, the experience of that love] what is the breadth and length and height and depth [of it];

[That you may really come] to know [practically, through experience for yourselves] the love of Christ, which far surpasses mere knowledge [without experience]; that you may be filled [through all your being] unto all the fullness of God [may have the richest measure of the divine Presence, and become a body wholly filled and flooded with God Himself]!

—EPHESIANS 3:17-19

In the Bible we see that Paul prayed for the church to really know the love of God by experience. Paul knew that a revelation of God's love was imperative, that people had to have it or nothing else in their lives was going to work properly.

Right relationships are based on love — love flowing both ways.

Once you begin receiving God's awesome unconditional love, you can begin not only loving Him in return, but you can also begin loving others.

GIVE AWAY WHAT YOU HAVE

In this is love: not that we loved God, but that He loved us and sent His Son to be the propitiation (the atoning sacrifice) for our sins.

Beloved, if God loves us so [very much], we also ought to love one another.

—1 JOHN 4:10,11

Having God's love in us, we can give it away. We can choose to love others lavishly. We can love them unconditionally as He has loved us.

Everyone in the world desires to be loved, to be accepted. The love of God is the most wonderful gift we are given. It flows to us, and then it should flow through us out to others.

I like to see myself as a dispensary of blessings. I want to be the type of person others can come to and have blessings dispensed into their lives. I want to make others happy, and I have discovered that as I do, I reap happiness in my own life.

For much of our lives, we try to find happiness the wrong way. We attempt to find it in getting, but it is found in giving.

Love must give; it is the nature of love to do so: *For God so greatly loved and dearly prized the world that He [even] gave up His only begotten (unique) Son, so that whoever believes in (trusts in,* clings to, relies on) *Him shall not perish (come to destruction, be lost) but have eternal (everlasting) life* (John 3:16).

We show love to others by meeting their needs — practical needs as well as spiritual needs. Generosity is love in action. Love is seen through edification and encouragement, patience, kindness, courtesy, humility, unselfishness, good temper, gentleness (believing the best) and sincerity.

We should actively pursue ways to show love, especially in little things.

LITTLE THINGS MEAN A LOT

"For who has despised the day of small things? . . ."
—ZECHARIAH 4:10 NKJV

Little things are often viewed as being insignificant, but in reality they are very important. I have found that little things are the spices in life.

We make a mistake if our only interest is in the main course (big things). The main course without spice is bland, tasteless and unsatisfying.

For example, a man may feel he is showing love for his family by working three jobs and bringing home plenty of money to assure them financial security. He is not home most of the time and is tired when he is there. He is doing a big thing but has no time for the little things like talking and laughing with the family, playing ball with his son, bringing home a rose for his wife, taking her to dinner, etc. He may end up with a divorce or at best a marriage that is unsatisfying, dull and tasteless. I repeat, it is the little things that are the spices of life.

LOVE IS THE SALT OF LIFE

> *You are the salt of the earth, but if salt has lost its taste (its strength, its quality), how can its saltness be restored? It is not good for anything any longer but to be thrown out and trodden underfoot by men.*
> —MATTHEW 5:13

In this verse Jesus tells us we are the salt of the earth, but if salt has lost its flavor it is not good for anything.

I say that all of life is tasteless without love.

Even acts of generosity done out of obligation but devoid of sincere love leave us empty. Love is the salt, the energy of life, the reason to get up every morning.

Every day can be exciting if we see ourselves as God's secret agents, waiting in the shadows to sprinkle some salt on all the tasteless lives we encounter.

For example, we might see a woman behind a counter in a fast food restaurant who looks unhappy, tired and angry. A simple thing like saying, "Your hair is really pretty," can add flavor to her day.

Love is an effort. Sometimes we allow ourselves to become lazy in dispersing this gift. I pray this book will charge your battery and help you get back to the main thing in life — *love!*

3

LOVING WITH WORDS

There are those who speak rashly, like the piercing of

a sword, but the tongue of the wise brings healing.

—Proverbs 12:18

Words have a tremendous impact on all of our lives.

I know people who have lived a life of crippling insecurity because their parents spoke words of judgment, criticism and failure to them on a regular basis. These people can be healed only by receiving God's unconditional love. They have been wounded in their souls (their inner selves, their mind, will and emotions), a place to which only God has total access.

Isaiah 61:1 says that Jesus came to bind up and heal the brokenhearted. He is the lover of our souls and through Him we can be secure and successful.

However, once people are wounded by the words of others, it takes time to overcome the wrong image they have of themselves.

That is why it is important that we learn to use our words for blessing, healing and building up and not for cursing, wounding and tearing down, as Ephesians 4:29 says: *Let no foul or polluting language, nor evil word nor unwholesome or worthless talk [ever] come out of your mouth, but only such [speech] as is good and beneficial to the spiritual progress of others, as is fitting to the need and the occasion, that it may be a blessing and give grace (God's favor) to those who hear it.*

That is especially true in regard to our own children.

WE REAP WHAT WE SOW

> *Train up a child in the way he should go [and in keeping with his individual gift or bent], and when he is old he will not depart from it.*
>
> —PROVERBS 22:6

As parents we should not tell our children they are something unless we want them to become what we are saying.

Words create an image inside of us, and Proverbs 23:7 says that as a person thinks in his heart, so is he.

If a parent tells a child he is stupid and can't do anything right, he will start producing the seed that is planted in him. Those negative words will have an effect on his perception of himself, which in turn will be manifested in his attitude and behavior. He will literally become what he believes himself to be based on what he has been told about himself.

The biblical principle is set forth in Galatians 6:7: . . . *For whatever a man sows, that and that only is what he will reap.*

We reap what we sow. Words are seeds, and they produce a harvest. Right words produce a harvest of good relationships. Likewise wrong words produce a harvest of bad relationships.

Some parents wonder why their children don't come to visit them very often once they are grown and out on their own. It may be because the children's memories of home are ones of nagging parents, faultfinders who used words to tear them down rather than build them up.

I have four grown children, and I am very glad that my husband and I sowed good words into their lives. We corrected them, but we were careful not to reject them. When they had difficulties, we always told them we believed in them and would always be there for them. Even when we did not like the things they did, and told them so, we emphasized that our "love" for them was an unchanging thing.

By the time Danny, our younger son, was born, we had a lot of God's Word in our hearts. I recall the Lord showing us never to say to Danny, "You're a bad boy!" We told him the wrong things he did were bad, but we never told him he was bad.

Many parents have the habit of using that phraseology to correct their children, but I believe it plants an image in them that they are bad. Those seeds produce an unwanted harvest of more bad behavior.

Generally speaking, if we believe in people, they will make a huge effort to live up to our confidence in them. We learned this through dealing with the employees in our ministry. We found that if we promoted someone we believed had potential, they would begin to act differently as soon as they were informed of their promotion. We have seen some employees start dressing more professionally and handle themselves in a more professional way. They work harder to become what we have told them we believe they can be.

Multitudes of people need someone to believe in them. They have been wounded by wrong words, but right words can bring healing in their lives.

One of our five division managers was once so fearful that she cried every time we tried to get her to do something new. She was afraid of me, afraid of life, afraid of failure — afraid of almost everything. Recently she told me, "Joyce, you believed in me more than I believed in myself."

Believing the best of people and speaking words that build them up is one way of loving them.

Think of these words and then think about how they make you feel:

Ugly	Stupid	Failure	Incompetent
Slow	Clumsy	Hopeless	

Do they make you feel uplifted, excited and happy, as though you can be a success at anything you attempt? I am sure they don't.

Now consider words like:

Attractive	Intelligent	Hopeful	Blessed
Creative	Talented	Anointed	

I am sure you find that such words affect you in a much more positive way.

Finally, read and consider these Scriptures in light of what we have been learning about the power of words:

Anxiety in a man's heart weighs it down, but an encouraging word makes it glad.

—PROVERBS 12:25

A man has joy in making an apt answer, and a word spoken at the right moment – how good it is!

—PROVERBS 15:23

Pleasant words are as a honeycomb, sweet to the mind and healing to the body.

—PROVERBS 16:24

Death and life are in the power of the tongue, and they who indulge in it shall eat the fruit of it [for death or life].

—PROVERBS 18:21

You can see why words are so important in the life of the person who truly desires to walk in love toward others.

MAKE LOVE A HABIT

And let us consider and give attentive, continuous care to watching over one another, studying how we may stir up (stimulate and incite) to love and helpful deeds and noble activities.

—HEBREWS 10:24

If we intend to make love a habit, then we must develop the habit of loving people with our words. The fleshly (lower, sensual) nature points out flaws, weaknesses and failures. It seems to feed on the negatives in life. It sees and magnifies all that is wrong with people and things. But the Bible says in Romans 12:21 that we are to overcome evil with good.

Walking in the Spirit (continually following the prompting or leading, guiding and working of the Holy Spirit through our own spirit instead of being led by our emotions) requires being positive. God is positive, and in order to walk with Him we must agree with Him. (Amos 3:3.)

It is easy to find something wrong with everyone, but love covers a multitude of sins: *Above all things have intense and unfailing love for one another, for love covers a multitude of sins [forgives and disregards the offenses of others]* (1 Peter 4:8).

Love does not expose faults; it covers them.

WATCH YOUR MOUTH!

> *But I tell you, on the day of judgment men will have to give account for every idle (inoperative, nonworking) word they speak.*
>
> —MATTHEW 12:36

Parents, employers, friends, husbands, wives, children — all of us need to make a commitment to love others with our words, to build confidence in others. Every word we speak can be a brick to build with or a bulldozer to destroy.

Choose your words carefully. Remember, words are seeds; they are containers for power. They are producing a good harvest or a bad harvest in your life and in the lives of those you love.

4

LOVING WITH MATERIAL GOODS

But if anyone has this world's goods (resources for sustaining life) and sees his brother and fellow believer in need, yet closes his heart of compassion against him, how can the love of God live and remain in him?

Little children, let us not love [merely] in theory or in speech but in deed and in truth (in practice and in sincerity).

—1 John 3:17,18

Many people love things and use people to get them. God intends for us to love people and use things to bless them. Sharing our possessions with others is one way to move love from the "talking-about-it stage" to the "doing-it stage."

God has given us a heart of compassion, but by our own choice we open or close it. As believers in Jesus Christ, God gives us His Spirit and puts a new heart (and mind) in us. Ezekiel 11:19 says that this new heart is sensitive and responsive to God's touch. There is something deep in every believer that wants to help others; however, selfishness can cause us to be so aggressive about obtaining our own desires that we become oblivious to the needs around us.

People are hurting everywhere. Some are poor; others are sick or lonely. Still others are emotionally wounded or have spiritual needs. A simple act of kindness like giving a pair of earrings or a tie to an insecure person can make that individual feel loved and valuable.

People can get caught in the trap of striving to have more prosperity; the struggle often produces little or no results. We should strive to excel in giving. If we do so, we will find that God makes sure we have enough to meet our own needs plus plenty to give away. (See 2 Corinthians 9:8.)

START WHERE YOU ARE

Do not say to your neighbor, Go, and come again; and
tomorrow I will give it. . . .

—PROVERBS 3:28

We can have good intentions and still be disobedient. Procrastination is very deceptive. We don't see it as disobedience because we intend to obey God; it is just that we are going to do it *when* — when we have more money, when we are not so busy, as soon as Christmas is over, after we get the kids in school this year, as quick as vacation is over, etc.

There is no point in praying for God to give you more money so you can be a blessing to others if you are not being a blessing with what you already have. Don't believe Satan's lies that you have nothing to give. Even if it is only a pack of gum or a ballpoint pen, start using what you have to bless others.

After I was filled with the Holy Spirit (received the divine power, ability and might of God to live the Christian life and fulfill His will) in February 1976, I began to experience a greater desire to give. Dave and I had been tithing since we were married, but we only did for others what we were obligated to do for birthdays, for Christmas, for other holidays and special occasions. It never occurred to us to "live to give," to excel in giving. We went to church every Sunday but had not been taught in these areas. We gave away things we did not want any longer, but not nice things we personally enjoyed or had more of than we needed.

We were not in a financial position to give more money than our 10-percent tithe, but the strong desire to give caused us to search for ways to do so anyway. So we gave away personal possessions, extra clothes, household items and an old car that we could have sold for a few hundred dollars but decided to pass on to a needy friend who used it for several years.

In the process of giving, we discovered that we did not have to have money to be a blessing to others.

START A BLESSING BOX

Get yourself a big box and start going through your possessions, asking God to show you what you have that you can use to bless others. Fill it up with things that are nice but that you are tired of, things you have duplicates of, things you bought because you once needed them but have not used for years.

For example, when my children were small I often needed a vaporizer during their winter colds or flu. As they got older it sat on a top shelf in our storage room in the basement. I brought it to my office, along with other items I was no longer using, and someone took it right away. Perhaps it was someone who knew a young mother who needed a vaporizer and could not afford one.

Look in cabinets, drawers, closets, the basement and the garage. You will fill your box up quickly. Don't keep something for years just in case you ever need it — if you're anything like me, by the time you need it, you will have forgotten you have it and go buy another one anyway.

Take the clutter that is frustrating you and turn it into blessings. Keep the box in a handy place and start asking God to show you who needs to be blessed.

One woman I know, who is a radical giver, got all the things together she wanted to use to bless people and displayed them on her kitchen table. She invited several friends over and told them to take anything on the table they wanted. She urged them to feel free to keep taking until everything was all gone.

I encourage you to be a giver and look for ways in which you can use what you have to be a blessing to others.

COMING UP HIGHER

For, as I can bear witness, [they gave] according to their ability, yes, and beyond their ability; and [they did it] voluntarily.

—2 CORINTHIANS 8:3

There are levels of giving; some are less painful than others. Giving away things we don't want or no longer use is good, but we should also give away new things, and things we have to make an effort to do.

If you know someone who has been through a difficult time, go shopping for that person; look for that special gift that you feel just right about. It may take some time, and for busy people that can be painful. It is good to purposely stretch yourself into new areas. Get out of the comfort zone with your giving.

Give away one of your favorites of some item; I can promise it will be painful. Why is it good to give until it hurts? Jesus did when He was willing to die on the cross for our sins (then He rose from the dead on the third day as God had promised), and I want to be like Him, don't you? As the saying goes: "NO PAIN, NO GAIN."

LOVE NOT THE WORLD

Do not love or cherish the world or the things that are in the world. If anyone loves the world, love for the Father is not in him.

—1 JOHN 2:15

Remember, love people and use things to bless them. That is hard for us to do if we love things excessively. You and I must strive to keep *things* in their proper place. We must not allow ourselves to put them ahead of people.

Sometimes people get so upset over the destruction or loss of a thing that they begin to mistreat others.

One day my previous housekeeper was cooking a roast for us in the pressure cooker. She did something wrong, and the valve blew off the top, shooting steam, roast, grease, potatoes and carrots straight up into the air. The ceiling fan above the stove was on full speed. It caught the food and grease and sent them flying all over the kitchen walls, ceiling, floor, furniture — and the housekeeper.

When I came home from work, she was sitting in a corner of the kitchen, crying. She looked so bad I thought she had received some tragic news. I finally got her to tell me what had happened, and when she did, I started laughing. By the time Dave came in, she and I were both laughing hysterically.

She said, "I've destroyed your kitchen!"

I remember telling her, "The kitchen can be replaced, but you can't. You're more important than the kitchen. Thank God you're not hurt."

There was a time in my life when that would not have been my response. Before I learned that people are more important than things, I would have become angry and said things to make the housekeeper feel stupid and guilty.

If we love people, God can replace things, but if we love things excessively, we may lose people who cannot be replaced.

Mercy (kind and compassionate treatment[1]) is one aspect of love. It is always wise to show mercy — because we often need it ourselves!

THINGS! THINGS! THINGS!

> *For we brought nothing into the world, and obviously we cannot take anything out of the world.*
> —1 TIMOTHY 6:7

Our society today is filled to the brim with commerce. Everyone is busy making money so they can buy more things. Sometimes it seems that we have shopping malls, mega malls or strip malls on every corner.

I marvel as I drive down the street and see the number of stores. I often say, "I don't know how all these stores can stay in business. It seems there wouldn't be enough shoppers to go around." I must be wrong because more and more stores are built every day.

Things in themselves are not evil, but they can become so if they lure us away from godly priorities: *For the love of money is a root of all evils; it is through this craving that some have been led astray and have wandered from the faith and pierced themselves through with many acute [mental] pangs* (1 Timothy 6:10).

God wants His children to be blessed. He wants us to have nice things. He delights . . . *in the prosperity of His servant* (Psalm 35:27).

The more we use our resources to be a blessing to others, the more God will bless us: *Give, and [gifts] will be given to you; good measure, pressed down, shaken together, and running over, will they pour into [the pouch formed by] the bosom [of your robe and used as a bag]. For with the measure you deal out [with the measure you use when you confer benefits on others], it will be measured back to you* (Luke 6:38).

Like Abraham, we are called by God to be blessed and to be a blessing: *And I will make of you a great nation, and I will bless you [with abundant increase of favors] and make your name famous and distinguished, and you will be a blessing [dispensing good to others]* (Genesis 12:2).

If our motive is to be a blessing, it proves God can trust us with money and things. We will reap what we sow; it is a spiritual law: *Do not be deceived and deluded and misled; God will not allow Himself to be sneered at (scorned, disdained, or mocked by mere pretensions or professions, or by His precepts being set aside). [He inevitably deludes himself who attempts to delude God.] For whatever a man sows, that and that only is what he will reap* (Galatians 6:7).

It is also a law of the universe: *While the earth remains, seedtime and harvest, cold and heat, summer and winter, and day and night shall not cease* (Genesis 8:22).

However, we should avoid giving with the singular motive of getting. Second Corinthians 9:6 states that we are to give (sow) generously . . . *that blessings may come to someone.* . . .

Blessing others should be our primary motive for giving.

Don't waste your life just making money and collecting things. As we have seen in 1 Timothy 6:7, we brought nothing into the world, and we will take nothing out of it, and in 2 Corinthians 9:9 we are taught that the deeds of the benevolent person will endure forever.

I want to leave something as a result of my journey through life. I refuse to pass through it as a "taker." I have decided to be a "giver." I want to bless people in tangible ways. I pray that you have the same desire.

EVERYONE NEEDS A BLESSING

As it is written, He [the benevolent person] scatters abroad; He gives to the poor; His deeds of justice and

*goodness and kindness and benevolence will go on
and endure forever!*

—2 CORINTHIANS 9:9

It is both good and scriptural to bless the poor. They should be one of our primary targets.

Look for people who are needy and bless them. Share what you have with those who are less fortunate than you are. But remember, everyone needs a blessing — even the rich, the successful and those who appear to have everything.

We often hear people say, "What do you buy the man or woman who has everything?" What to buy or do for them is not the real issue; it is the act of love that is needed.

Dave and I recently felt led by God's Spirit to make a monthly financial commitment from our ministry outreach fund to a well-known, successful Christian music artist. He wrote back saying the gift was very timely and that in twenty-three years of service no national ministry had ever become a partner with him.

Everyone loves this man. He is a tremendous blessing to the entire body of Christ. Why had no other national ministry ever reached out to him financially? I believe it is because we have been trained to give to the poor or needy, but have had little or no instruction regarding the needs of the middle or upper class, the successful or rich in the world.

They have emotional needs the same as other people, and sometimes even greater needs because they normally carry a heavy load of responsibility. They are usually the providers, those who take care of other people, those who minister to their needs. As a result, they are seldom seen as people who are in need themselves.

Everyone needs a blessing. We all need to be encouraged, edified, complimented and appreciated. We all get weary at times and need other people to say to us, "I just wanted to let you know that I appreciate you and all you do." That can be done with words alone, but it is also a very nice gesture to add a material or monetary gift when appropriate. We often hear the phrase "money talks," and so it does.

I believe God blesses us so we can be a blessing — not only in a few places, but everywhere we go!

Start using what you have to be a blessing, and your well will never run dry.

When you are blessed, I am sure you don't want others to think there is no need to give to you because you are already being blessed. So remember to sow into the poor and the rich, the downtrodden and the successful. (See 2 Corinthians 9:6,7).

I have learned to enjoy a variety of seed planting. I love to give to those in need and help bring them up to the level on which I am living. I also love to give to those who are enjoying a level of life to which I would like to be promoted.

If you want your ministry to grow, find a few larger ministries you respect and sow into them. If you want your marriage healed, sow into the life of someone who has a great marriage, releasing your faith with your seed for a harvest in that area. If you want your finances to increase, sow into the needs of others.

Actually, the possibilities are endless.

If you live to meet needs and to make others happy, you will find "joy unspeakable" in the process. (See 1 Peter 1:8 KJV.)

5

LOVING WITH THOUGHTS

For as he thinks in his heart, so is he. . . .

—PROVERBS 23:7

We make a mistake when we have the opinion that our thoughts don't affect people. We can often feel the thoughts of others, and they can feel our thoughts.

Our thoughts not only affect others, they also affect us in a most amazing way. Proverbs 23:7 teaches us that as we think, so we are. If we think unkind thoughts, we become unkind. If we think loving thoughts, we become loving. If we think angry thoughts about a certain individual for a period of time and suddenly find ourselves in his presence, we discover that it is virtually impossible for us to treat him in a loving way.

BRINGING THOUGHTS INTO CAPTIVITY

For the weapons of our warfare are not carnal but mighty in God for pulling down strongholds, casting

down arguments and every high thing that exalts itself
against the knowledge of God, bringing every thought
into captivity to the obedience of Christ.

—2 CORINTHIANS 10:4,5 NKJV

Satan tries to fill our minds with wrong thoughts all the time. Our responsibility is to cast down those wrong thoughts, get them under control and replace them with right thoughts.

We must choose our thoughts carefully because they affect us and consequently the people around us.

The following testimony, sent to me several years ago, clearly illustrates the power of thoughts and why we must learn to exercise control over them.

"During Christmas I moved a fig tree upstairs to the bedroom to make room for the Christmas tree. It had a small branch with about a dozen leaves on it down below the rest of the branches. It didn't look right, ruining the shape of the tree.

"When I would wake up in the morning, I'd see that tree in the window and think, 'I'm going to cut that branch off.' Every time I passed that tree I'd think, 'That branch doesn't look right; I'm going to get rid of it.'

"Time went by, and the tree was moved back to the living room. I continued to think a negative thought each time I noticed it. All total this lasted about a month and a half.

"One morning I walked by the tree, and every leaf on that little branch was yellow. There was not one other yellow leaf on the whole tree. I got kind of goose bumpy and told my husband. He looked at me and said, 'I'm sure glad you think nice things about me!' I cut that branch off that day!

"I have always had a difficult relationship with my mother-in-law. Of course I never thought I had any blame, being so sweet and all. I decided that this was worth an experiment. Every time I thought about my mother-in-law, I determined to bless her — to go out of my way to think about her and bless her!

"She seldom calls me or has any interest in chatting with me, but within five days she had called me three times, just for a moment, but they were friendly calls! She hadn't called me more than six times the whole last year. So I ordered your series 'The Power of Thoughts,' and I watch what I think about people now."

It would appear this woman's thoughts actually killed the branch of that tree and changed her mother-in-law's attitude toward her! Isn't that amazing?

THOUGHTS MINISTER DEATH OR LIFE

> For to be carnally minded is death, but to be spiritu-
> ally minded is life and peace.
> —ROMANS 8:6 NKJV

We want to minister life to others with our thoughts, not death.

Romans 8:6 tells us the mind of the flesh is death, but the mind of the Spirit is life. Negative, ugly thoughts minister death to us as individuals and also to others, while positive, loving, beautiful thoughts minister life.

Here is an example from my own life that taught me how our thoughts affect the people around us.

I was shopping with my younger daughter one day when she was a teenager. On that particular day her hair was very messy, and her face was broken out. She had just started wearing makeup and was still learning how to apply it properly. As a result, she had too much on, and it did not look good.

Each time I looked at her I thought, *You look really bad today.* After some time went by, I noticed she was looking depressed, and I wondered what was wrong with her, so I asked.

"I feel really ugly today," she replied.

When she said that, God spoke in my spirit and said, "See what your thoughts have done to her?"

I was immediately convicted that my thoughts had been wrong and very displeasing to the Lord.

Often we think things about people we would never say to them, not realizing that even our thoughts can affect others. We can sin in thought, word or deed, so we should be careful in all of these areas.

OUR THOUGHTS AFFECT OUR ATTITUDE

[Let your] love be sincere (a real thing); hate what is evil [loathe all ungodliness, turn in horror from wickedness], but hold fast to that which is good.

Love one another with brotherly affection [as members of one family], giving precedence and showing honor to one another.

—ROMANS 12:9,10

If you and I allow our thoughts about a person to be negative, our attitude toward that individual will also be negative. If we want to love people, we must make a decision to think good thoughts about them.

I cannot imagine Jesus being nice to someone while thinking bad thoughts about him. We shouldn't do that either. As previously stated, our love must be sincere. If we are praying for an individual to change, while thinking constantly about what he is like and how he will probably never change, our prayers will be negated by our negative thinking.

It is important for us to have a loving attitude toward people, an attitude that is filled with mercy and kindness. A right attitude begins with right thinking.

When I notice my attitude toward a person or a situation going in a wrong direction, I always find that the problem began with wrong thinking. I have learned that in order to avoid thinking negatively, I must keep my thoughts and attitude renewed daily. (Ephesians 4:23.)

THINKING GOOD THOUGHTS ON PURPOSE

And be constantly renewed in the spirit of your mind
[having a fresh mental and spiritual attitude].
—EPHESIANS 4:23

A real breakthrough came for me in my own love walk when I realized that love was something I needed to do on purpose. I could not wait to feel loving; I had to choose to be loving. The same rule applies to our thoughts. We must learn to think good thoughts about people on purpose.

We must learn to look for the good in everyone, not the evil. We all have faults and weaknesses, but we all also have things about us that are good.

I admit that we must look harder to find the good in some people than in others, but to be like Jesus, that is what we must do.

Jesus finds the good in everyone and magnifies it instead of the bad. He found the good in me and started developing it until it finally surpassed a lot of the things that were wrong with me. He has done the same thing in the lives of many of us, and He expects us to do the same for the people we encounter on a daily basis: *Beloved, if God loved us so [very much], we also ought to love one another* (1 John 4:11).

Take a moment and try this experiment. Just sit and think some good thoughts on purpose about someone you know, and see how much better you feel yourself. If you keep it up, you will begin to notice changes in that person's attitude toward you. One reason that individual will change is because you will have changed.

Thinking good thoughts opens the door for God to work. If we want the Lord's good plan to manifest in our life, we must get into agreement with Him (Amos 3:3). He is not negative in any way, and according to the Bible, we have been given the mind of Christ (see 1 Corinthians 2:16) — *but we must choose to use it.*

We also have a mind of the flesh, and I often feel it is like the earth's gravitational pull; if we don't resist it, we are pulled in its direction.

If I drop my hairbrush, it will fall to the earth because gravity pulls it down; however, I can interrupt the fall of that brush by quickly reaching out and catching it with my hand. The gravitational pull is just as strong as it was before, but I have the power to resist it and not allow the hairbrush to fall to the ground.

We might look at our thoughts in the same way. Because of the sinful nature of man, our thoughts will automatically go in a negative direction unless we direct them otherwise.

When a person accepts Jesus Christ as Savior, he is born again. In other words, his spirit is renewed (made new). Second Corinthians 5:17 KJV states that when anyone is in Christ, he is a new creature; old things pass away, and all things become new.

Out of the renewed (born-again) spirit, every other area of our lives can experience newness of life. It is a process that requires breaking old habits and forming new ones, but persistence pays off.

If you have not been working with the Holy Spirit to break old thought patterns and form new ones, it is time to get started. Think some good thoughts about people on purpose, and as your attitude starts to change toward them, watch your relationships start to change for the better.

LED, GUIDED AND CONTROLLED
BY THE HOLY SPIRIT

> . . . you are living the life of the Spirit, if the [Holy] Spirit of God [really] dwells within you [directs and controls you]. . . .
>
> —ROMANS 8:9

When love takes charge of us (which is another way of saying, when God takes charge of us), we cannot think bad things about people. We don't even want to.

We are not really living the life of the Spirit until we allow the Holy Spirit to control every area of our life. He will certainly never get control of our life until He has control of our thoughts and words.

Being led by the Spirit is central to a victorious Christian life. As long as we think our own thoughts and speak our own words, we will never experience victory.

Each of us has a purpose in the earth. If God had no purpose for us, He would take us out of the world as soon as we accept His Son Jesus Christ as Savior so we could begin right away enjoying heaven and living in His Presence. But the fact is, God does have a purpose for each of us, and we should learn what it is and cooperate with it.

Learning God's purpose for us is easy; it is written throughout the pages of the New Testament. God wants to use each one of us who is His child to encourage someone else to become His child (to turn his life over to Jesus by inviting Him to be his Savior). It does no good to talk to people about Jesus unless we are living a Christian lifestyle to back up our words. Thoughts have everything to do with the process.

Our life is a reflection of our thoughts. It is impossible to have a good life unless we have trained ourselves to have good thoughts. If we want others to see Jesus reflected in our life, then His mind must be reflected in us.

We must be led by the Spirit in our thinking; that is where all Spirit-led living begins. If we want others to see and desire what we have, if we are to make them hungry and thirsty for God as the Bible teaches us to do, then our life must be lived in such a way as to accomplish this goal.

Far too many people go to church every Sunday, but cannot be identified as Christians the rest of the week.

God is not satisfied with our punching a time clock on Sunday morning, giving Him one hour, and then clocking out until the next Sunday.

In the same way, it is not pleasing to God when we think wrong thoughts about others. (1 John 4:20,21.) Judgmental, critical, negative thoughts are not pleasing to God: *So then those who are living the life of the flesh [catering to the appetites and impulses of their carnal nature] cannot please or satisfy God, or be acceptable to Him* (Romans 8:8).

We have the freedom to choose what will control us. We can either let the mind of the flesh control us, or we can chose the Holy Spirit and His way of thinking.

THE FLESH OR THE SPIRIT?

So then, brethren, we are debtors, but not to the flesh [we are not obligated to our carnal nature], to live [a life ruled by the standards set up by the dictates] of the flesh.

For if you live according to [the dictates of] the flesh, you will surely die. But if through the power of the [Holy] Spirit you are [habitually] putting to death (making extinct, deadening) the [evil] deeds prompted by the body, you shall [really and genuinely] live forever.

—ROMANS 8:12,13

I am sure that many people who will read this book have been controlled all of their life by wrong thinking. They think all their problems are caused by the devil, other people, the way they were raised as children, etc. But the truth is that in many cases the problem is simply a lack of knowledge or a lazy spirit that refuses to act on the knowledge available.

Thinking right thoughts will often resemble warfare. The mind is the battlefield on which Satan tries to defeat us. In the Bible we are told to "cast down" wrong thoughts, but what does that mean? It means once wrong thoughts present themselves to us, we are to refuse to receive them and turn them over and over in our mind. We are not to give them strength by meditating on them.

The real key to victory is not only to cast down wrong thoughts, but to replace them with right ones: *For the rest, brethren, whatever is true, whatever is worthy of reverence and is honorable and seemly, whatever is just, whatever is pure, whatever is lovely and lovable, whatever is kind and winsome and gracious, if there is any virtue and excellence, if there is anything worthy of praise, think on and weigh and take account of these things [fix your minds on them]* (Philippians 4:8).

It is virtually impossible to think two things at the same time. When a new thought comes in, the old must go.

Go ahead, try it! Start thinking about your name for example. Now begin to think about your address. When you changed to thinking about your address, you stopped thinking about your name.

We get rid of the darkness by turning on the light. In the same way, we rid ourselves of wrong thoughts by deliberately turning our attention to right thoughts.

Be determined to love God, yourself and others with your thoughts. Ask the Lord to reduce you to love. It is the only road to true happiness, and the only way we can be a witness in our world today.

6

LOVE IS WILLING TO ADAPT AND ADJUST

Live in harmony with one another; do not be haughty (snobbish, high-minded, exclusive), but readily adjust yourself to [people, things] and give yourselves to humble tasks. Never overestimate yourself or be wise in your own conceits.

—ROMANS 12:16

One of the most important facets of love is unselfishness, which is characterized in this Scripture as the willingness to adapt and adjust to the needs and desires of others.

People who have been reduced to love are not selfish. They have learned to be adaptable and adjustable to others. Selfish people, on the other hand, expect everyone around them to adjust to them, but they themselves are often unable to do that for others without becoming angry or upset.

Learning to adapt and adjust myself to the needs and desires of others was very difficult for me. To be honest, I just plain wanted my way, and I got upset when I did not get it.

I was selfish!

That is not the trademark of a true Christian, as we see in the life of the apostle Paul.

LOVE IS SELF-SACRIFICING

> *For although I am free in every way from anyone's control, I have made myself a bond servant to everyone, so that I might gain the more [for Christ].*
>
> *To the Jews I became as a Jew, that I might win Jews; to men under the Law, [I became] as one under the Law, though not myself being under the Law, that I might win those under the Law.*
>
> —1 CORINTHIANS 9:19,20

Paul walked in love and taught his disciples to do the same. He learned to adapt himself to others so that he might win them for Christ. He had obviously learned that saving another person's soul was more important than having his own way.

If more people would learn that lesson, I sincerely believe there would be a lot more dedicated Christians in the world today.

Paul was able to adapt himself to others because he made the decision to do so for the sake of Christ. As a result, I believe he became sensitive to what people needed from him and tried to give it to them. As believers, we should be willing to do the same.

Not all people need the same thing from us. One of our children, for example, may need more of our personal time than another one does. One of our friends may need more encouragement on a regular basis than another. Our sister may need us to be a good listener, while our brother may need us to talk to him.

That does not mean that we are to allow the needs of others to run our life; the Holy Spirit should have that privilege. But it does mean that we should deposit ourselves with God and trust Him to take care of us while we make it our business to take care of others.

My aunt needs me, my parents need me, my brother needs me, my husband needs me, each of my four children needs me, my five grandchildren need me, my employees need me, my partners need me, my friends need me — they all need me in a different way.

Do I ever feel too needed? Yes, once in a while I do, but I remind myself that God gives me grace for whatever He places in my life, and that I am blessed to be loved and needed.

Do I ever get weary of always trying to be available to meet the needs of others? Yes, but I remind myself of all the selfish years I lived and how unhappy I was; when I do that, it does not take long for my attitude to get adjusted.

I don't allow people to control me, but I do attempt to meet their needs that are reasonable. My aunt and my parents need me to call them and/or see them at least once a week, so I do that for them. That is one way I can express my love for God and for them.

Telling people "I love you" is rather weak if we don't go beyond that and attempt to meet their needs.

My husband needs to play golf once a week if at all possible, so I try to make sure our schedule gives him that opportunity. He really enjoys watching sports, and although I don't enjoy that at all, I manage to occupy myself once or twice a week while he settles down and watches a ball game or a golf tournament.

I remember all the years when I did not want him to do those things because I wanted him to do what I wanted to do. I became angry if he watched a ball game on television or went to play golf. I was miserable because I had not learned to adjust myself to his needs. I wanted him to adjust to my needs and desires, but I was not willing to adjust to his.

In many other areas he did adjust to my desires. He almost always allowed me to choose the restaurants we ate in, when we had friends over, how often we went out and many other things.

For years I never saw what he did, only what he did not do, and it was ruining our relationship. I am glad I learned to adapt and adjust. It was a little hard on my flesh for a while, but it probably saved my marriage.

It is easier for some to adapt than others, but we must all learn to do it.

My general manager and friend has a God-given temperament which lends itself to adapting to others. She does not have strong opinions about things like what to watch on television or where to go eat. One thing suits her as well as another. When we spend a day together for entertainment, she is happy with whatever I choose. For example, she does not really enjoy shopping herself, but she is happy to go with me and be patient all day while I try on clothes or shoes.

One of our daughters has a similar personality; whatever I want to do is usually all right with her. Our other daughter is more particular about what she does. For example, she does not like to shop a lot unless she needs to buy something. I like to shop, and she has the choice to go along with me anytime she desires, but I don't feel hurt or rejected if she chooses not to go.

I respect my two daughters' different personalities and try to have a relationship with them that meets all of our needs — theirs and mine.

I have two sons. One of them needs a lot more of my time than the other one does. One is independent and enjoys being home with his family. The other is totally the opposite. He likes to be with people, and I am glad his dad and I are two of the people he likes to be with.

I learned a long time ago that it does no good to try to get a person to be something he is not.

I love all of my children equally, and I have different relationships with each of them. All of them are our good friends as well as our children. They all work for the ministry, which means we have a lot of different relationships to keep separated, but God gives us the grace to function together as a team and respect each other's rights and personalities.

All of us are very opinionated, but we have learned not to try to force our thoughts and views on each other. We realize that everybody needs some space and wants to be free to do things as he or she sees fit.

A person who has been reduced to love has no trouble establishing and maintaining good relationships with people because his primary goal in life is to make others happy. As we will see in the next chapter, love is not selfish, it does not demand its own way or rights. (1 Corinthians 13:5).

LOVE SHOWS RESPECT

Render to all men their dues. [Pay] taxes to whom taxes are due, revenue to whom revenue is due, respect to whom respect is due, and honor to whom honor is due.

—ROMANS 13:7

Love respects the differences in other people. A selfish person expects everyone to be just the way he is and to like whatever he likes.

Respecting individual rights is very important. If God had wanted us to all be alike, He would not have given each of us a different set of fingerprints. I think that one fact alone proves that we are created equal, but different.

We all have different gifts and talents, different likes and dislikes, different goals in life, different motivations, and the list goes on and on.

Love shows respect; the person who loves has learned to give freedom to those he loves.

Freedom is one of the greatest gifts we can give. It is what Jesus came to give us, and we must also give it to others.

As your children get older, let them make some choices for themselves. When they are grown, don't try to run their lives any longer. If they make decisions you don't agree with — even wrong decisions — respect their right to do so.

Before judging others, we should remember all the bad decisions we made in our earlier years.

Our younger son made some decisions right after he was married that my husband and I did not agree with, but we respected his right to make them. When things did not work out well as a result of his decisions, we did not go to him and say, "If you had listened to us, this would not have happened."

"I told you so" is not the way to build good relationships.

Our son's bad decisions cost him some time and money, but it was not the end of the world. He learned an important lesson about taking a little more time before making decisions. His bad decisions turned out to be valuable after all because he learned from them.

We showed him love by showing him respect. First, we showed respect by not judging his decisions; second, we showed respect by not saying "I told you so."

A partial definition of the word *respect* from Noah Webster's 1828 *American Dictionary of the English Language* states that it means "to view or consider with some degree of reverence; to esteem as possessed of real worth."[1]

All of God's creation has great worth and should be treated as such. Since people are the height of His creation, they should be treated with great respect and considered very valuable.

Recently, an employee told me that the manager of his department never showed him the courtesy of knocking at his door, but simply barged in and interrupted him no matter what he was doing. He said, however, that the supervisor of the department showed more respect and always knocked before entering.

Sometimes such disrespectful behavior is caused by a wrong attitude. If a person sees himself as "the boss" and others as "under" him, he may feel he has a right to do such things. However, if he changes his attitude and begins to treat others the way he wants to be treated (Matthew 7:12), he will do things much differently than he's used to doing them.

A boss may need to interrupt an employee from time to time, and he does have that right, but how he does it is very important. There is always a respectful and a disrespectful way to handle every situation.

Many people never have their gifts and talents used in life because they never learn to respect authority, family, friends or even their possessions.

I heard this story and I want to share it with you to illustrate my point.

Two very famous college football coaches had just addressed a large gathering. After their speeches they opened the meeting for questions. A high school coach in the audience asked, "What is the highest priority in your recruiting of young men to come play at your universities?" He thought surely the answer would be speed, size, strength or intelligence, but none of these were the correct answer.

The coaches' answer surprised everyone. They said that before choosing a possible candidate for their teams, they wanted to know how much respect the boy showed his parents because if he respected his parents, he would also respect others and be able to become an effective part of a winning team.

Respect is an attribute that must always supersede talent and ability. Over the years there have been some very talented people in our ministry whom we have not been able to promote because they did not have proper respect for authority or for their co-workers.

In Romans 12:16, Paul tells us to live in harmony with others by being willing to adjust ourselves to them. He goes on to talk about humility saying, . . . *give yourselves to humble tasks. Never overestimate yourself or be wise in your own conceits.*

People who think more highly of themselves than they should find it difficult, if not impossible, to adjust to others. Their inflated opinion of themselves causes them to see others as "little" and "unimportant."

This kind of attitude is very dangerous because it hides in our thinking. It causes us not to respect the opinions and ideas of others, therefore, making it impossible for us to be part of a team of any kind.

Many people who are gifted in the area of leadership have strong, aggressive personalities. They are highly goal-oriented and accomplishment-motivated. They often mistreat others without even realizing they are doing so. They simply feel they are getting the job done, which to them is the most important thing.

A leader should definitely operate in love because what is on the head flows down to the body. (Psalm 133:2.) The leader sets the example for others. Anyone in a leadership position automatically becomes a teacher. He teaches others what is right and wrong by his actions. If he shows disrespect to employees, they will in turn show disrespect to one another.

LOVE GIVES PREFERENCE TO OTHERS

Love one another with brotherly affection [as members of one family], giving precedence (prefer-ence) and showing honor to one another.

—ROMANS 12:10

Giving preference to others requires a willingness to adapt and adjust. It means to allow them to go first or to have the best of something.[2]

Because we travel so much by air, Dave and I and the members of our travel team accumulate a lot of frequent flyer miles which can be cashed in for first-class accommodations on later flights. Since there is limited space in the first-class section, there are often more people in our group than can be seated there on any given flight.

The rule at the airport is "first come, first served." There are times when our employees arrive at the airport ahead of us and get first-class seats, and there are none left for Dave and me. Whenever this happens, the employees always insist that Dave and I take the first-class seats while they sit in the coach section. By so doing, they are loving us by giving us preference. They prefer for us to have the comfort of first class above themselves. They show us honor and respect through their act of love.

These kind of things really help build good relationships.

Our employees won't allow us to carry anything heavy when we are traveling with them. Someone always grabs our bags. It is not that we are any better than they are, but they are showing respect for our position in the ministry and expressing love for us.

We have had employees who never offered to carry anything and who even appeared insulted if they were asked to do so, which let us know right away that their spirit was all wrong. Anyone who wants to be a leader in the kingdom of God must be willing to be a servant. (Matthew 23:11.)

We show preference when we give someone else the best cut of meat on the platter instead of keeping it back for ourselves. We show preference when we allow someone with fewer groceries in his cart than we have in ours to go in front of us at the supermarket checkout counter, or when we are waiting in line to use a public restroom and someone behind us in line is pregnant or elderly and we choose to let that individual go ahead of us.

Each time we show preference we have to make a mental adjustment. We were planning to be first, but we decide to be second. We are in a hurry, but we decide to wait on someone else who seems to have a greater need.

A person is not yet rooted and grounded in love until they have learned to show preference to others. (See Ephesians 3:17 NKJV.)

We have multiple opportunities to adapt and adjust almost every day. If we are locked into our plans, we will have a difficult time doing so. It is good to have plans. Without plans we won't accomplish much. We should stick to our plans if at all possible. If we don't stay focused, we will never stay on track. However, we are out of balance if we cannot discern when we need to stick to our plans and when we need to adapt and adjust to accommodate something important that comes up unexpectedly.

Don't just learn to adjust, but learn to do it with a good attitude. Learning to do these things is learning to walk in love.

Remember, love is not just words; it is action and is seen in all of our behavior.

7

THE MANY FACETS OF LOVE

Love endures long and is patient and kind; love never is envious nor boils over with jealousy, is not boastful or vainglorious, does not display itself haughtily.

It is not conceited (arrogant and inflated with pride); it is not rude (unmannerly) and does not act unbecomingly. Love (God's love in us) does not insist on its own rights or its own way, for it is not self-seeking; it is not touchy or fretful or resentful; it takes no account of the evil done to it [it pays no attention to a suffered wrong].

It does not rejoice at injustice and unrighteousness, but rejoices when right and truth prevail.

Love bears up under anything and everything that comes, is ever ready to believe the best of every person, its hopes are fadeless under all circumstances, and it endures everything [without weakening].

Love never fails. . . .

—1 CORINTHIANS 13:4-8

In Chapter 6 we saw that unselfishness is an important facet of love. But love is like a diamond; it has many facets. Whichever way a diamond is turned, it sparkles in a little different way. That is the way love is.

Love is one thing, but it is displayed in many different ways. If we are not aware of this fact, we may believe that we are walking in love while being impatient or rude, selfish or proud.

Love is displayed in practical ways; it is what holds relationships together. How many marriages would be saved if a husband would simply be kinder or a wife would be less touchy? What would happen if all the members of a church would decide to believe the best of one another and of their pastor?

The thought is quite sobering.

We should not imagine that we know anything of love unless we are operating in all the facets of love. These fruit of the Spirit (defined in Chapter 1) should be our goal.

Once my goal was to build a big ministry; yet no matter what I did, my ministry did not grow. I had my priorities out of order. Developing my love walk was toward the bottom of my list; therefore, God would not permit growth in my ministry. I needed to be educated on the real meaning of love. I discovered quickly that it was more than words. I learned that it was costly and that it took quite an effort.

Let's consider some of the many facets of love presented in the "love chapter" — 1 Corinthians 13.

LOVE IS PATIENT

Love endures long and is patient. . . .

—1 CORINTHIANS 13:4

Love is seen as we are patient with one another.

The world today is filled with impatient people. It seems that everyone is in a hurry. Stress levels are very high in the life of most people, and the pressure they live under provokes impatience. Even Christians are as prone to impatience as everybody else.

Most of us don't want to wait for anything. We are always in a hurry to get on to the next thing on our busy schedule; therefore, we get impatient with anyone who holds us up or slows us down.

You and I have many weaknesses ourselves, yet we get impatient with the faults and weaknesses of others. We want God to be merciful to us, but often we are not willing to give to others the same mercy we receive.

We are impatient with people and we are impatient with our circumstances. We are even impatient with God. We want Him to move faster than He does. We want Him to give us what we want right now whether we are ready to handle it or not.

We want to reap all the benefits of the spiritual life, but we are not willing to do what it takes to develop spiritual maturity.

We don't want to go through anything. We want to bypass all the rough roads in life, even though the difficult times help us grow spiritually. We want "drive-through breakthroughs." In other words, we want and want and want, yet are not willing to mature. We want all of our breakthroughs to come quickly, without any preparation or effort on our part.

We can go through the drive-through lane of a fast-food restaurant and order a quick hamburger, but it does not have the nutrition that a healthy home-cooked meal does. Thousands of people today are suffering from poor health. The root cause of much of it is poor nutrition which has resulted from grabbing something quick to eat so we can get on to the next thing on our agenda. Multitudes are also suffering from spiritual malnutrition, caused by being in too big a hurry to spend time with God.

Love is patient. It is not in a hurry. It always takes time to wait on God, to fellowship with Him.

A person whose life is marked by love is patient with people. He is even patient with himself, with his own frailties and weaknesses. He is also kind. He takes the time to listen to the elderly person who is lonely and wants to talk. He is willing to listen to the same story four or five times just to show kindness.

The patient person is long-suffering. He can put up with something uncomfortable for a long period of time without complaining. He has the power to endure whatever comes with good temper.

James 1:4 KJV tells us that the patient man is . . . *perfect and entire, wanting nothing.* That means he is content.

If we are impatient, Satan can keep our lives in turmoil. All he needs to do is arrange for us to have a situation we don't like, and our peace goes out the window. He sets us up to get us upset!

Patience is a wonderful virtue. It is one facet of love which must be developed by the person who is seeking to have a strong love walk and display the character of Jesus Christ.

LOVE IS NOT ENVIOUS OR JEALOUS

. . . love never is envious nor boils over with jealousy. . . .
—1 CORINTHIANS 13:4

According to Proverbs 14:30, *. . . envy, jealousy, and wrath are like rottenness of the bones.*

In the Word of God, we are commanded not to covet anything that belongs to another person. (Exodus 20:17.) We are not to be envious or jealous because these things poison our own life and hinder loving relationships with others.

Love does not envy or become jealous. It rejoices when others are blessed.

I have discovered the best way to get over envy or jealousy is to admit it. When you begin to feel jealous or envious, be honest with God and ask Him to help you live free from it.

I must admit, there are times when I hear about a blessing that someone has received, and I start to think, *When is that going to happen to me?* When that thought enters my mind, I immediately open my mouth and say, *I am happy for him. If God can do it for him, He can do it for me too.*

If a young woman is unmarried and has been praying and asking God to give her a husband, it may be difficult for her to be truly happy for her friends when they get married.

In such situations, instead of being unhappy or jealous or envious, we can be happy for others and let their blessing be an encouragement to us, believing that what God did for them, He can do for us. If He did it once, He can do it again!

We should learn to pray for other people to be blessed. We should learn to pray for God to do for them what we are believing He will do for us. What we make happen for someone else through our prayers, etc., God will make happen for us.

We should bless others and not be afraid they will get ahead of us. We must not envy anyone else's appearance, possessions, education, social standing, marital status, gifts and talents, job or anything else because it will only hinder our own blessing.

There was a time in my life when I envied people who could sing really well. God showed me that by envying them, I was unable to enjoy the gift He had placed in them for my benefit.

You see, God puts gifts in us for others, not for ourselves. A singer may enjoy singing tremendously, but she does not enjoy it as much as those who hear her. God gave her the gift for the benefit of others.

I enjoy preaching and teaching the Word very much, but I probably don't enjoy it as much as the people who are helped by my gift of communication. It does others more good than it does me. I am helped through the gifts of others, and they are helped by my gift.

That is one reason that we are all different and need each other. Being jealous and envious of one another is a total waste of time. We all have gifts that God has given us; they don't come from any other source. We must be content with what heaven has sent us. God has a unique plan for each of our lives, and the gifts He gives us are part of that plan. We can trust Him; He knows His business. What He does for others is actually none of our business. Our business is to walk in love.

Honestly ask yourself if there is anyone in your life that you are jealous or envious of. If there is, begin to deal with that situation.

Love is not envious, nor does it boil over with jealousy. Anyone who intends to have a strong love walk will have to grow beyond being envious and jealous of other people.

LOVE IS NOT PROUD AND BOASTFUL

Love . . . is not boastful or vainglorious, does not display itself haughtily.

It is not conceited (arrogant and inflated with pride). . . .
—1 CORINTHIANS 13:4,5

Love does not think more highly of itself than it should, simply because the person who is walking in love is not thinking of himself at all. His mind is not on himself, but on others.

Love is always reaching out, looking for ways to be a blessing, ways to serve God. Love takes every opportunity to do good and is always mindful to be a blessing to others, as we are told in Galatians 6:10: *So then, as occasion and opportunity open up to us, let us do good [morally] to all people [not only being useful or profitable to them, but also doing what is for their spiritual good and advantage]. Be mindful to be a blessing, especially to those of the household of faith [those who belong to God's family with you, the believers].*

The person who is walking in love has no difficulty saying "I'm sorry," but the proud man or woman finds these two simple words very difficult to utter.

Pride strives to be seen as knowing more than others; in contrast, love does not display its knowledge, nor does it seek to appear "right" in every debate.

Paul tells us that knowledge without love only causes people to be puffed up: *Now about food offered to idols: of course we know that all of us possess knowledge [concerning these matters. Yet mere] knowledge causes people to be puffed up (to bear themselves loftily and be proud), but love (affection and goodwill and benevolence) edifies and builds up and encourages one to grow [to his full stature]* (1 Corinthians 8:1).

The proud individual boasts of his accomplishments. He fails to give God the glory, but takes it unto himself. He is frequently found talking about himself — what he is doing, what he has done, what he knows, who he knows, etc.

The Bible warns us against boasting:

> *Do not boast of [yourself and] tomorrow, for you know not what a day may bring forth.*
>
> *Let another man praise you, and not your own mouth; a stranger, and not your own lips.*
>
> —PROVERBS 27:1,2

> *Yet you do not know [the least thing] about what may happen tomorrow. What is the nature of your life? You are [really] but a wisp of vapor (a puff of smoke, a mist) that is visible for a little while and then disappears [into thin air].*

You ought instead to say, If the Lord is willing, we
shall live and we shall do this or that [thing].

But as it is, you boast [falsely] in your presumption
and your self-conceit. All such boasting is wrong.

—JAMES 4:14-16

The apostle Peter is a good example of a man who had to be humbled.

In Matthew 26:31-35 we see that Peter thought more highly of himself than he should have. In that passage, we read that just before the crucifixion Jesus told His disciples they would all be offended and fall away from Him. In verse 33, Peter declared to the Lord that he would never do such a thing. In response, Jesus warned Peter that before that very night was over, his fears would cause him to deny Him three times, but Peter could not conceive that he would ever be that weak.

Peter really did not know himself, and many of us are the same way. We look at others and judge them, thinking, *I would never do that.* Then when we find ourselves in a similar situation, we do things we would have never believed possible.

Peter needed to go through the experience of failing, of falling apart in the crisis hour. He had to see his weaknesses before he could bring them to the cross and find God's strength.

Yes, Peter failed miserably. He denied Jesus three times. He fell apart in a crucial time, but the end result was good. The experience humbled him and brought him to the place where God could use him greatly.

God can only use humble men and women. We must humble ourselves and He will exalt us. (1 Peter 5:6.)

I have heard it said that it is yet to be seen what God can do through a man or woman who will give Him all the glory.

Pride and love do not mix. Love is not proud and haughty. It is not boastful or vainglorious. It is not puffed up. Love does not look down on others; it does not see them as little and insignificant. Because love values every person, everyone who comes in contact with someone who is full of love will be made to feel special, valuable and built up.

Pride is a difficult problem for us to deal with because it hides — it hides in our thinking, in the deepest recesses of our mind. Pride will not admit that it is present because it is too proud to do so.

We have had teaching tapes available for years on the subject of pride. They are not our best sellers. I believe that is because those people who need them are too proud to pick them off the tape table to purchase. After all, someone might see them and wonder if they have a problem with pride.

Jesus continually humbled Himself, and we must follow His example:

> Let each of you esteem and look upon and be con-
> cerned for not [merely] his own interests, but also
> each for the interests of others.
>
> Let this same attitude and purpose and [humble]
> mind be in you which was in Christ Jesus: [Let Him
> be your example in humility].
>
> —PHILIPPIANS 2:4,5

As with Peter, the Lord had to teach me many lessons about pride, and they were hard lessons to learn.

It is quite amazing how interested we are in ourselves. It is a powerful testimony when the Holy Spirit can work with us and change us from proud, haughty, puffed up, boastful individuals, into humble servants of God and man.

I am still growing in these areas and probably always will be, but I am pressing on toward the mark of His high calling. (Philippians 3:14 KJV.)

The high call of God is that we should be like Jesus, that Christlikeness should be developed in our character.

Jesus humbled Himself and came to the earth as the Son of Man to save us from our sins. We cannot help others unless we are willing to follow His example and humble ourselves.

The Bible states that Jesus stripped Himself of all His rightful privileges as the Son of God and became a servant. (Philippians 2:6,7.)

Pride must be served, but humility is free to serve others. Pride demands its rights, but humility willingly lays them aside when needed. Pride lives for self, but humility lives for others.

The person who is committed to walking in love will grow to hate pride in himself. Every appearance of it in his life will be dealt with immediately because he knows the danger of it.

What is the danger of pride?

Pride keeps people trapped in a prison called "self." There are only three people in this prison: "Me, Myself, and I." It is a really lonely place.

Pride hinders God from using people. It is mean to others, shows disrespect, is stingy and always demands to be first in everything. Pride wants to be seen, noticed, pampered, made comfortable and exalted.

Humility is satisfied knowing that God is in control. It trusts, enjoys rest and peace. It is obedient and joyful and delights in making others happy.

LOVE IS NOT RUDE

> . . . it is not rude (unmannerly) and does not act unbecomingly. . . .
>
> —1 CORINTHIANS 13:5

It amazes me how much rudeness we encounter in our daily lives. I would like to say that it all emanates from unbelievers, but the fact is that many Christians are rude.

We believers are in the world, but we must resist becoming like it, or perhaps I should say, work to get over being like it.

Although we become followers of the Lord Jesus Christ and begin to study God's Word and ways, we still have a lot of bad habits. Those bad habits need to be broken and new ones formed. It takes time, but we should be relentless in our pursuit of godly behavior.

Those who walk in love are not rude and unmannerly. They do not behave themselves unbecomingly.

If I am dressed unbecomingly, it means that I am wearing something that does not look good on me. When we as believers act unbecomingly, we are wearing spiritual clothing that does not look good on us. God is not impressed with our closets full of outfits, but He is impressed when we "put on love." (Colossians 3:14.) To put on love, we must put on behavior that is not rude.

It is rude to interrupt others when they are talking, especially without saying, "Please excuse me, but I really need to ask you something important." It is rude to push in front of others to be first in line or to get the best seat. It is rude to yank something out of someone's hand or to fail to say "thank you" and "please."

It is rude to stand outside someone's open office door when it is clear that person is having a conversation with someone else. In such a case, we can say, "I need to see you for a moment when you have time," then get far enough away that we are not overhearing the conversation.

It would behoove all of us to get a good book on manners and read it often. I am sure that the list of good manners would be helpful and that the list of rude manners would be endless. Let us all ask God to show us the ways in which we are rude and unmannerly and then ask Him for the grace (as I told you previously, grace is God's unmerited favor) to change.

LOVE IS NOT SELF-SEEKING

. . . Love (God's love in us) does not insist on its own rights or its own way, for it is not self-seeking. . . .
—1 CORINTHIANS 13:5

The nature of love flows out; it does not turn in.

Selfishness is rampant in our world today, and we must not let it rule us. Everywhere we look, we see messages that we should be more concerned about ourselves than about other people. I see signs that say such things as:

"Buy yourself a new car, you deserve it."

"If you don't take care of #1, who will?"

"Take a trip to the Bahamas, you owe it to yourself."

There is nothing wrong with doing things for ourselves; in fact, we need to. But there is something desperately wrong when we allow ourselves to become obsessed with ourselves, our desires and needs.

It seems we are always fighting for "our rights." Perhaps for a change we should fight for someone else's rights: the unborn child, the physically impaired, the hungry, the elderly and others like that.

In Matthew 24 Jesus' disciples asked Him what would be the sign of His coming and the end of the age. In verse 12 He warned that in the last days . . . *the love of the great body of people will grow cold. . . .*

I have seen this verse fulfilled in my own lifetime, and probably so have you. People don't care about others the way they once did. Materialism has crept into the church. People no longer have time to help others, to serve others, to pray for others; they are often too busy trying to get what they want for themselves.

Haggai 1 introduces us to a group of people who had ignored an instruction from God for eighteen years. They had been told to rebuild the temple, yet they said, . . . *The time is not yet come that the Lord's house should be rebuilt [although Cyrus had ordered it done eighteen years before] (v. 2).*

They had spent those years trying to build their own houses, and they found themselves in desperate circumstances. They never had enough money. Things were not working out right for them. Whatever they did obtain they quickly lost it.

God spoke to them through the prophet Haggai and said, . . . *Consider your ways (your previous and present conduct) and how you have fared (v. 7)*. In other words, "Look at your situation and ask yourselves why you are in such dire straits; it is because you are trying to take care of yourselves instead of obeying Me and working together to provide something for everyone. It won't work!"

Selfishness will not work. It stops up every avenue of blessing that would otherwise flow into our life.

Selfish people are always quite miserable and usually think if they could just get what they want, they would feel better. Satan has them on a treadmill of striving to make themselves happy and never succeeding.

All through the Bible men and women were warned about the danger of being selfish and encouraged to remember to reach out to others in love and service:

> *Depart from evil and do good; and you will dwell forever [securely].*
> —PSALM 37:27

> *For he who sows to his own flesh (lower nature, sensuality) will from the flesh reap decay and ruin*

and destruction, but he who sows to the Spirit will
from the Spirit reap eternal life.

—GALATIANS 6:8

Do not forget or neglect to do kindness and good, to be
generous and distribute and contribute to the needy
[of the church as embodiment and proof of fellow-
ship], for such sacrifices are pleasing to God.

—HEBREWS 13:16

Once when Jesus was teaching a crowd of people which included His disciples, He told them that if they or anyone else wanted to follow Him, they must forget themselves, they must lose sight of themselves and all of their own interests. He said this was their cross to carry. (Mark 8:34.)

Our cross is not poverty and a life filled with disaster; it is living unselfishly. Walking in love is costly, and it is an effort; for this reason many people never step out onto the same path that Jesus walked.

As we have already seen, love is adaptable and adjustable; it does not demand its own way.

Psalm 37:5 KJV is the Scripture that my mother-in-law wrote in the front cover of my first Bible, which she gave me many years ago: *Commit thy way unto the Lord; trust also in him; and he shall bring it to pass.*

Over the years, I have had to apply that portion of Scripture to many situations in my life because I was the kind of person who wanted my own way. I was like a wild horse that must be broken before it is of any value to anyone. I fought with life for a long time before I finally had to commit "my way" to the Lord.

Although it was hard to give up my way, I learned to simply believe that if things did not go as I had planned or desired, it was because God had a higher purpose in mind, as He tells us in Isaiah 55:9: *For as the heavens are higher than the earth, so are My ways higher than your ways and My thoughts than your thoughts.*

Instead of struggling continually, always trying to make arrangements to get my way, I learned to pray the same prayer that Moses did: *Now therefore, I pray You, if I have found favor in Your sight, show me now Your way . . .* (Exodus 33:13).

Just try to practice being totally unselfish, even for one day, and you will quickly find what a challenge it is.

The flesh is strong, but the Spirit is stronger. The Holy Spirit lives in our spirit, and He will enable us to walk in His fruit if we feed on the Word of God and spend time in His Presence, in prayer and fellowship.

I am certainly glad that what is impossible with man, is possible with God. (Matthew 19:26.)

LOVE TAKES NO ACCOUNT OF THE EVIL DONE TO IT

> *. . . it is not touchy or fretful or resentful; it takes no account of the evil done to it [it pays no attention to a suffered wrong].*
>
> —1 CORINTHIANS 13:5

Love forgives; it does not hold a grudge. It is not touchy, easily offended, nor is it fretful or resentful. Some people get their feelings hurt about everything. It is very difficult to be in a relationship with people like this. Touchiness needs to be overcome. Once again, it keeps us centered upon ourself and what others are doing to us or not doing for us.

We have many opportunities every day to get offended; each time we must make a choice. If we choose to live by our feelings, we will never flow in this all-important facet of love.

I once read that 95 percent of the time when people hurt our feelings, it was not what they intended to do. We always seem to assume people are attacking us, while the truth is, most of the time they are not even interested in us, let alone staying up nights trying to figure out ways to offend us.

If we don't forgive quickly, but keep records of how others have hurt us, sooner or later the list will get so long that we can no longer be in relationship with those people.

That kind of touchiness, fretfulness and resentment is what causes many divorces. I recently read that it is estimated that 50 percent of first marriages[1] and 60 percent of second marriages[2] now end in divorce. That would not happen if people would learn the facets of love and abide by them.

Selfishness is driving many to the divorce court, as is unforgiveness. Many of the best "record keepers" are people with a pride problem. They count up everything others do wrong, but fail to realize that in many instances, they do the same things they are judging others for doing. (Romans 2:1.)

In the early years of our marriage, each time Dave and I got into an argument I brought up everything he had ever done to displease me since day one. It absolutely amazed him. He would say, "I can't even remember that. Where do you keep all this information?"

Because I was unable to simply forgive and let any offense go, I kept it in me, meditated on it regularly and had quick recall when I needed some ammunition to make Dave feel bad.

Actually I was full of poison. I was trying to have a relationship with God, not realizing that I had to leave my gifts at the altar when I came to worship until offenses were removed that were between me and my fellowman. (Matthew 5:23,24.) Prayer was a waste of time for me because my faith would not work as long as I refused to forgive others. (Mark 11:24-26.)

Bitterness makes our life bitter, our attitude bitter, our words and thoughts bitter. We resent the blessings of those we have not forgiven. We even sometimes get mad at God because He is blessing them, when we feel He should be punishing them.

"Drop it, leave it and let it go," is what *The Amplified Bible* says we are to do with offenses. (Mark 11:25.) It is important to forgive quickly. The quicker we do it, the easier it is. A weed that has deep roots is harder to pull out than one that has just sprung up.

God is love, and He forgives and forgets. If we want to be like Him, then we must develop the same habit.

All those with whom we have a relationship will hurt us at times; it is impossible for them not to. We must remember that we are human beings and not put pressure on one another to be absolutely perfect. God forgives us and is glad to do so:

He has not dealt with us after our sins nor rewarded us according to our iniquities.

For as the heavens are high above the earth, so great are His mercy and loving-kindness toward those who reverently and worshipfully fear Him.

As far as the east is from the west, so far has He removed our transgressions from us.

—PSALM 103:10-12

Let's follow the Lord's lead and get to the point where it is almost impossible to offend us.

I don't want to waste any more of my time being upset; it is not worth it. I am at the point in my life that I have already lived more years than I have left. I don't intend to waste them being touchy, fretful or resentful.

What about you?

LOVE ALWAYS BELIEVES THE BEST OF EVERYONE

Love bears up under anything and everything that comes, is ever ready to believe the best of every person, its hopes are fadeless under all circumstances, and it endures everything [without weakening].

—1 CORINTHIANS 13:7

This facet of love is what enables us to walk in the previous one we just mentioned.

How can you and I refuse to be offended unless we are willing to believe the best of those who have hurt us. We can choose to believe the worst (that they did the thing that hurt us on purpose), or we can choose to believe the best (that they did not mean the thing the way we perceived it).

Our thoughts seem to go something like this: "What if I believe the best, and they really did hurt me on purpose? If that is so, I surely don't want them to get away with it."

The thing that has helped me most in this area is the realization that I am really the one helped by choosing to believe the best of everyone, even if I am wrong in my assessment of them.

A wise person does what he can to help himself, to make his life more enjoyable. Being offended never really injures the offender; it only makes the one who was offended miserable. Often the offender is off somewhere enjoying himself, not even aware that he has offended someone.

The quicker we learn to turn people and situations over to the Lord, the quicker we can start enjoying a peaceful, fruitful life. God is our Vindicator; we cannot vindicate (defend or justify) ourselves. When we try to, we only make matters worse. Whoever hurt us may not be able to pay us back, but God can and will, if we trust Him. Part of trusting is obeying His commandment to forgive:

> *For we know Him Who said, Vengeance is Mine [retribution and the meting out of full justice rest with Me]; I will repay [I will exact the compensation], says the Lord. And again, The Lord will judge and determine and solve and settle the cause and the cases of His people.*

It is a fearful (formidable and terrible) thing to incur
the divine penalties and be cast into the hands of the
living God!

—HEBREWS 10:30,31

Let us begin to behave as if we believe the Bible. In it, God tells us over and over what to do about our enemies — love them, pray for them, bless and do not curse them, give the situations to Him and He will bring justice. (Luke 6:35; Matthew 5:44 KJV.)

We function too much on feelings. When we are offended, we say, "You hurt my feelings." That is exactly right; our feelings got hurt, but we don't have to live by feelings. Adverse feelings will always show up to run our life, but thank God we have the fruit of self-control. The flesh does not have to control us; we can (through the power of the Holy Spirit) control it.

Sow mercy and you will reap mercy; sow judgment and you will reap judgment. Start sowing forgiveness. You may need some yourself some day.

LOVE DOES NOT REJOICE AT INJUSTICE AND UNRIGHTEOUSNESS

It does not rejoice at injustice and unrighteousness,
but rejoices when right and truth prevail.

—1 CORINTHIANS 13:6

Love is grieved at injustice. It always wants what is fair and right. It craves justice, not only for itself, but especially for others.

I don't like to see people mistreated. I have been hurt a lot in my life, and I well remember how it feels.

We should care about others and their pain, pray for them and do what we can to relieve their suffering. Love is not unfeeling; it cannot look at unjust situations and just simply not care or do nothing.

The worldly mentality of "don't bother me with it, that is your problem" has no place in the life of Christians. Obviously, we cannot physically or financially fix everyone's problem, but we can care. We can work with the Holy Spirit to make sure we don't allow our heart to become hardened by all the violence and injustice all around us.

Television continually brings murder, rape, accidents, starvation of children and every ungodly atrocity into our living rooms. We must guard against becoming so accustomed to it that it no longer touches us in our feelings. Love does not rejoice when unrighteousness prevails.

I am grieved by our whole society today. I crave to see right actions, godly governments, excellence, integrity, craftsmanship, quality, marriages that last, children who are loved and properly cared for, etc. I pray I never get so used to the way things are that I begin to flow downstream with them.

Hearing of a violent murder does not affect us the way it did thirty years ago. Dave says when he was a boy, his family heard for the first time ever of a paperboy who had been robbed. Everyone was horrified that such a thing could happen. Today we might think, "Robbed? Is that all? He's lucky he didn't get killed!"

God is love, and He loves righteousness (knowing you are right with God — acting right, talking right, etc.) — therefore, those who walk in love must also love righteousness. Psalm 97:10 states that if we love the Lord, we must hate evil. Those who love righteousness are often persecuted for it — Jesus was, and we are not above our Master. (Matthew 10:24.)

You may work in an environment that is filled with evil and unrighteousness, bad language, gossip, hatred, envy, greed, immoral relationships, etc. If you take a stand for righteousness, you may be made fun of, talked about unkindly or even totally rejected. But love never fails. Keep walking in love, hating injustice and unrighteousness, and the favor of God will come upon your life in an astounding way, as the Lord has promised: *"Blessed are those who hunger and thirst for righteousness, For they shall be filled"* (Matthew 5:6 NKJV).

Don't hate evil people, just their evil ways. God hates sin, but He loves sinners. Don't compromise and sink to the level of others just to win their favor. The favor of God is so wonderful; it cannot be compared to the favor of man.

In the Bible, we read about godly people such as Daniel and Joseph, who had the favor of God on their life.

Daniel was surrounded by evil and unrighteous people, but he refused to compromise. He loved righteousness, and God gave him favor, which caused him to become a powerful government official in the kingdom of Babylon. (Daniel 1,2,6.)

Joseph was mistreated; however, he maintained his integrity. He loved righteousness. He did not hate his brothers, but he hated what they did to him. God gave him favor, and he rose to a position of power in Egypt second only to that of Pharaoh. (Genesis 37; Genesis 39-41.)

In this instance, Egypt could represent the secular world and Pharaoh the boss. When God promotes you, your fellow employees won't make fun of you any longer.

LOVE NEVER FAILS

The God-kind of love bears up under anything and everything that comes. It endures everything without weakening. It is determined not to give up on even the hardest case. The hard-core individual who persists in being mean can be eventually melted by love.

It is hard to keep showing love to someone who never seems to appreciate it or even respond to it. It is difficult to keep showing love to those individuals who take from us all we are willing to give, but who never give anything back.

We are not responsible for how others act, only how we act. Our reward does not come from man, but from God. Even when our good deeds seem to go unnoticed, God notices and promises to reward us openly for them: . . . *your deeds of charity may be in secret; and your Father Who sees in secret will reward you openly* (Matthew 6:4).

If a person quits and gives up the task God has assigned him because no one is noticing him, he is not serving God from a pure heart. For example, if a woman feels that God wants her to work in the nursery each week at church but quits two months later because not one mother has even thanked her, she was not doing the job to love God and others, but to get love for herself.

This kind of honesty is hard to swallow sometimes, but it is nonetheless true. We must never give up because the demands of love are too hard.

I am so glad that God did not give up on me. How could He? He is love, and love never quits. It is always right there, doing its job. Love knows that if it refuses to quit, it will ultimately win the victory: *And let us not lose heart and grow weary and faint in acting nobly and doing right, for in due time and at the appointed season we shall reap, if we do not loosen and relax our courage and faint* (Galatians 6:9).

I realize that some people may refuse to receive our love no matter what we do. They treat God the same way. That does not mean that love has failed. Love upholds us. It gives us joy. It pleases God when we walk in love. Love always has more positive results than anything else.

Don't fail to walk in love because love never fails!

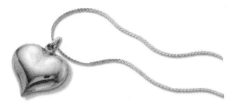

8

UNCONDITIONAL LOVE

For I am persuaded beyond doubt (am sure) that
neither death nor life, nor angels nor principalities,
nor things impending and threatening nor things to
come, nor powers,

Nor height nor depth, nor anything else in all creation
will be able to separate us from the love of God which
is in Christ Jesus our Lord.

—Romans 8:38,39

To fully understand all the different facets of love, we must talk about the two kinds of love: the God-kind of love and man's love.

Man's love fails, gives up; but God's love does not. Man's love is finite, comes to an end; but God's love is infinite and eternal. Man's love is dependent on favorable behavior and circumstances; God's love is not. People place conditions on their love, but God's love is unconditional.

LOVE IS UNCONDITIONAL

But God shows and clearly proves His [own] love for us by the fact that while we were still sinners, Christ (the Messiah, the Anointed One) died for us.

—ROMANS 5:8

According to God's Word, He loved us before the world was formed, before we loved Him or believed in Him or had ever done anything either good or evil.

God does not require us to earn His love, and we must not require others to earn ours. We must realize that love is something we are to become; it is not something we do and then don't do. We cannot turn it on and off, depending on who we want to give it to and how they are treating us.

As believers in Jesus Christ, the love we are to manifest to the world is the unconditional *love of God* flowing through us to them. We don't receive God's love and then try to give them ours. Our love has conditions and limits; His does not.

Loving people unconditionally is a very big challenge. I would be tempted to say it is impossible, but since God tells us to do it, surely He must have a way for us to do it. He never commands us to do something and then leaves us to perform it on our own. He does not throw us the football, so to speak, and then say, "Now you make the touchdown." His grace (His power, ability and favor as we have said previously) is sufficient for us (2 Corinthians 12:9), meaning that He enables us to do what He has called us to do.

Sometimes we pray to be able to love the unlovely, and then do our best to avoid every unlovely person God sends our way. Some people are sent into our lives for the sole purpose of being sandpaper to us. Not only do others have rough edges, but so do we. Learning to walk in love with unlovely people and learning to be patient in trials are probably the two most important tools God uses to develop our spiritual maturity.

Believe it or not, all those obnoxious people in our lives help us. They sharpen and refine us for God's use.

LOVE IS BEYOND MERE KNOWLEDGE

[That you may really come] to know [practically, through experience for yourselves] the love of Christ, which far surpasses mere knowledge [without experience]. . . .

—EPHESIANS 3:19

We cannot understand the God-kind of love with our minds. As we have seen in Ephesians 3:19, it far surpasses mere knowledge. Often it seems unfair. If we try to reason it out, we will surely lose it.

I can find no real reason why God should love me and use me in His kingdom. If I look for reasons to love others, I will probably not find a great number of people I can love. But God does not operate that way; He doesn't look for people who are worthy of His love. His love is unconditional. He looks for people who are in need of His love. That's why He chose me — and you.

Unconditional love unselfishly loves selfish people, generously gives to stingy people and continually blesses unappreciative people.

Unconditional love thinks long range. It sees what people can become if only someone will love them. It is stronger than anything else; it can reach into and bring healing to places that no natural medicine could ever reach.

It was definitely the love of God that overcame the evil in my life, that changed me and drew me into a deep relationship with Him. It is that same love flowing through us to others that will change them.

Loving people unconditionally is a good thing, and according to Romans 12:21, it is with good that we are to overcome evil. Change takes time, and we must be willing to suffer with another through those difficult times of being transformed.

Because Dave loved me unconditionally, he was willing to suffer with me while God was changing me. I had never seen real love. I did not even know what it was. Everyone who had ever said they loved me had hurt me and used me. I needed to see love; just hearing the words was not sufficient.

Most people who are hard to love have suffered so much pain along the road of life that it has altered their personality. Outwardly they may seem hard and bitter, but inwardly they are crying out for love.

That was the case with me. Outwardly I acted as if I needed no one, yet inwardly I was starving for love.

LOVE IS UNCHANGING

For I am the Lord, I do not change. . . .
—MALACHI 3:6

Real love, God's love, is the same all the time; it never changes. *It just is!*

No wonder when Moses asked God what he should say to the Israelites when they asked him who had sent him to Pharaoh on their behalf, God answered, "I Am. . . ." (Exodus 3:13,14.)

I am more than willing to admit that I have not yet arrived in this area of unconditional love, but I certainly want to learn it, and I believe you do too. As human beings it seems we are ever changing, we must learn to be more stable.

Stability was a trait I began to notice in Dave after we got married. I had never really been in the presence of stable people. Dave was just the same everywhere, all the time. He was not one way when he left for work in the morning and another way when he came home from work in the evening. His circumstances did not change his behavior.

He did not come home and treat the children and me badly if others had mistreated him during the day. Being in a traffic jam for two hours did not make him grouchy. Feeling bad physically did not make him grouchy. Even when I was grouchy, it rarely made him grouchy. He was just the same.

God had worked with Dave for years prior to our marriage and had developed stability in his character.

Stability must be worked in us. As we go around and around the same mountains in life, we finally learn not to let them upset us. Then and only then are we candidates for showing God's love to a needy world.

If we have not learned to be stable during difficult circumstances, we will not be able to show stability with difficult people.

LOVE CORRECTS AND DISCIPLINES

For the Lord corrects and disciplines everyone whom
He loves. . . .

—HEBREWS 12:6

Even though true love itself is unconditional, there are many things in life that must have conditions placed on them.

Our employees receive a raise in pay each year if they have performed their duties well and have been what I call "low maintenance employees." If they do not perform properly, are excessively late and absent, constantly ask for things outside the company guidelines, must be corrected often about excessive personal phone calls, etc., they do not get a raise, but a reprimand. If their bad behavior were rewarded, they would never learn to behave any better.

If a student does not do his classwork, refuses to study, and misses class regularly, he is not promoted to the next grade. If he were, he would keep those bad habits all of his life.

Correction and discipline are not evidence of a lack of love. As a matter of fact, the willingness to correct and discipline properly is a clear sign of love.

In the beginning of our ministry when my love walk was less developed, I was not as long-suffering as I am now. If someone really angered me, I would loudly declare to Dave or our general manager how I was going to handle the situation: "I tell you, I'm not going to put up with this! By tomorrow morning that person will no longer have a job!" etc., etc.

After I had finished blowing off steam and had calmed down, God would then tell me that I was not going to do any of what I had said. In fact, He would tell me that I was going to correct that person in love and give him another chance, just as He had done for me for so many years.

Love works through problems with people if at all possible.

There are people on our staff right now I would have fired two months after they started had God not stopped me, especially in the early days of my ministry. Now many of those same people are some of our most valued employees.

We all have possibilities; we just need someone to work with us. Most of us are stubborn, and we don't give in right away. For this reason, love must have a long-range attitude. It must be willing to invest, and often for long periods of time, with no visible return on the investment.

Dave loved me unconditionally for many years before I even wanted to change. Most of those years I thought everyone had a problem but me. I actually thought Dave was wimpy because he was not combative. Now I know that weak people are combative; strong people walk in love.

Dave was more of a man than I would ever meet again in my life, and I almost lost him at one point in our relationship through my stupid, stubborn, ungodly ways.

God gave me exactly what I needed when He gave me Dave Meyer. It may be that you have been given exactly what you need also, but you just need to recognize it. Or you may be in a relationship with someone who needs you. You may be the strong one, and your mate may need to receive unconditional love from you.

If so, do it for Jesus. Do it because He has done it for you. Do it gladly and willingly. Ask Him for strength to do it, and above all, remember that true love, unconditional love, the God-kind of love, never fails.

LOVE OVERCOMES AND TRANSFORMS

Do not let yourself be overcome by evil, but overcome
(master) evil with good.

—ROMANS 12:21

A mean, evil individual can be completely transformed by regular, persistent doses of God's love. Because people's religious experiences in many cases have been unfulfilling to them, they have never entered into a relationship with Jesus Christ that is personal enough for them to begin receiving His healing, transforming love.

Religion often gives people rules to follow and laws to keep. It can even lead them to believe they must earn God's love and favor through good works. That is the exact opposite of true biblical teaching.

God's Word says, *We love Him, because He first loved us* (1 John 4:19), and that . . . *mercy triumphs over judgment* (James 2:13 NKJV). It is the goodness of God that leads men to repentance (Romans 2:4), not the keeping of laws and rules.

Religious organizations often teach people what to do, but fail to teach them how to do it. Many people have tried religion and discovered it did not change them or their life at all.

Jesus frequently spoke against the religious leaders of His day. He said some very stern things about them — and to them:

> *They tie up heavy loads, hard to bear, and place them on men's shoulders, but they themselves will not lift a finger to help bear them.*
>
> —MATTHEW 23:4

> *Woe to you, scribes and Pharisees, pretenders (hypocrites)! For you give a tenth of your mint and dill and cummin, and have neglected and omitted the weightier (more important) matters of the Law – right and justice and mercy and fidelity. These you ought [particularly] to have done, without neglecting the others.*
>
> —MATTHEW 23:23

> *Woe to you, scribes and Pharisees, pretenders (hypocrites)! For you are like tombs that have been whitewashed, which look beautiful on the outside but inside are full of dead men's bones and everything impure.*
>
> —MATTHEW 23:27

When I use the term "religion," I am not casting stones at any particular denomination or independent church. Any of these can have "religious people" in them. As a matter of fact, all of them do.

Jesus did not come to give man religion; they already had that before He came. He came to give man a deep personal relationship with the Father, through Him.

People need a relationship with God, not a religion.

If a young man is in prison because he never knew the love of a father, never had a relationship with his father, how is religion (the following of rules and regulations) going to help him? His own father probably had many rules and regulations, but never spent enough time in relationship with the young man to teach him how to keep them. Telling people what to do is simply not enough; we must show them.

I regret to say that many of the religious people I have known in my life did not show me love. They did, however, show me rejection, criticism and judgment.

Religious people love conditionally; they love those who are just like them. Anyone who is different from them frightens them. They cannot love the young boy with long hair and baggy bluejeans with holes in the knees. They tell him he must change to be part of their group. They can't love the ex-prostitute who just received Christ as Savior, but has not yet learned how to dress properly.

Religious people want everyone to "clean up." The problem is, their definition of "clean up" differs widely. Some want you to cut your hair, while others tell you if you cut your hair, you're living in sin. Some want you to look your best, while others tell you if you want to look nice, you're vain. They are all different, but rarely do any of them accept people the way they are. They don't know how to hate sin and love sinners.

I hate a religious attitude because it is always full of pride, criticism and judgment.

As I said at the beginning of this section, many needy people have tried religion and found it to be an empty experience. They thought that by going to a church somewhere on Sunday morning they would find God. Some churches are full of God, but sad to say, others are not.

It grieves me when I think of how many people are looking for worldly answers to their problems simply because they tried religion and were met with rules, laws, rejection, judgment and no love.

Unconditional love does not allow people to remain the same; instead, it loves them while they are changing. The ex-prostitute does need to learn how to dress in a godly manner, but if she feels rejected before she learns, she may well run right back to her old lifestyle. The homosexual who desperately wants to be set free must feel loved and accepted while he is breaking out of his bondage.

Unconditional love will overcome sin and transform lives.

A good friend of mine, Pastor Don Clowers from Dallas, Texas, told me a sad story with an awesome ending.

A young man attended one of his campmeetings several years ago and made a profession of faith at the altar. The young man was a homosexual, and even though he had accepted Christ as his Savior, he continued to fall back into his old lifestyle. He truly wanted to be free, but his addictive lifestyle had a strong hold on his mind and emotions.

People who are repentant and sincerely want to be free are totally different from those who want others just to accept them and their sinful lifestyle.

Pastor Clowers began to feel that God wanted his wife and him to take this young man into their home and let him live there while he was being delivered. They kept him for a year. They prayed with him, counseled him, loved him unconditionally, corrected him and helped him in every way they knew how. During this year on a few occasions he fell back into sin, but they persisted in working with him because they could see that he was sincere in his desire to be free. Today that young man is married and serves as pastor of a good church — he was totally set free.

I don't believe a brand of religion that does not include unconditional love could have done that.

Jesus said that He did not come for the well, but for the sick. (Matthew 9:12.) Our world today is sick, from head to toe, and there is no answer for what ails it except Jesus Christ and all that He stands for.

God loves all people, but many of them may never know it unless Christians everywhere begin to pray and ask the Lord to reduce them to love.

9

LOVE IS IMPARTIAL

And Peter opened his mouth and said: Most certainly and thoroughly I now perceive and understand that God shows no partiality and is no respecter of persons.

—ACTS 10:34

If love is unconditional, then it must not show partiality.

This does not mean that we cannot have special friends or that we cannot be involved with certain people more than others. It means that we cannot treat some people one way and other people a different way. We cannot be kind to those who are good friends with us, and not care how we treat those who are of no interest or importance to us.

I know many people with whom I would not be interested in having a deep personal relationship, because I know that, for one reason or another, it would not be fruitful for either of us. That does not mean these people are bad; it just means a casual relationship between us would be better than a close relationship.

All of us need certain things from our close friends, and not all people are able to give it to us. God has what I call "divine hook-ups" for all of us — people who are "in the same flow," as we are.

God has given me several people like that in my life, and I appreciate them very much. But He has also taught me to treat everyone with respect, to make them feel valued, to listen to them when they are talking to me and not to judge them in a critical way.

Our love walk can readily be seen by how we treat people who cannot do us any good, people with whom we are not interested in developing a relationship.

I remember an incident in which God taught me a lesson in this area.

I had taken our son to the doctor to have a cast removed from his arm which he had broken. While I was waiting, an elderly man came and sat down next to me. He wanted to talk, but I wanted to read. He kept telling me how he had fallen on the ice and hurt his leg, and how much this doctor had helped him.

I must admit, I just wanted him to be quiet. I really paid no attention to him or showed him any respect. I was somewhat aware that he was lonely and probably had very few people to talk with, but I was not willing to be his blessing for that day.

The Holy Spirit spoke in my heart and said, "How would you treat this man if he were a famous preacher you would like to get to know?"

I was cut to my heart at those words. I immediately knew that I would hang onto every word, smile, make compliments and do all kinds of things to help me establish a relationship — in short, all the things I was *not* doing for this man who meant nothing to me.

This kind of behavior is not acceptable for anyone who desires to be reduced to love.

At the time, I was praying about walking in love, but I really did not come close to realizing what that would mean to my life and behavior.

Loving others frequently requires sacrifice. It requires that we put others first, doing what benefits them, and not just us.

As we saw earlier, the Word of God tells us that He does not show partiality, that He is no respecter of persons. It also tells us many times that we are not to be a respecter of persons (be prejudiced, show partiality or practice favoritism).

LOVE IS NO RESPECTER OF PERSONS

> . . . for there is no distinction between Jew and Greek. The same Lord is Lord over all [of us] and He generously bestows His riches upon all who call upon Him [in faith].
>
> —ROMANS 10:12

> My brethren, pay no servile regard to people [show no prejudice, no partiality]. Do not [attempt to] hold [and] practice the faith of our Lord Jesus Christ [the Lord] of glory [together with snobbery]!
>
> For if a person comes into your congregation whose hands are adorned with gold rings and who is wearing splendid apparel, and also a poor [man] in shabby clothes comes in,

And you pay special attention to the one who wears the splendid clothes and say to him, Sit here in this preferable seat! while you tell the poor [man], Stand there! or, Sit there on the floor at my feet!

Are you not discriminating among your own and becoming critics and judges with wrong motives?

—JAMES 2:1-4

If indeed you [really] fulfill the royal Law in accordance with the Scripture, You shall love your neighbor as [you love] yourself, you do well.

But if you show servile regard (prejudice, favoritism) for people, you commit sin and are rebuked and convicted by the Law as violators and offenders.

—JAMES 2:8,9

In our ministry, we sometimes give special seating to specific people attending our conferences, but not because they are either rich or poor, well dressed or poorly dressed. We may give a special seat to a pastor we know in the area, because the Bible says that we are to give honor to whom honor is due. (Romans 13:7.) Or we may set aside a special seating area for relatives of those on our travel team. Our travel team works very hard all year, and this is one way we can show them honor and appreciation. But we may also provide special seating for those in wheelchairs, the hearing impaired or others with special needs.

We don't call our partners in that area who have given a large amount of money to the ministry and offer them special seating, while ignoring the ones who are faithful each month with a smaller offering.

To be honest, to remain impartial takes some soul-searching. The flesh has tendencies toward prejudice and partiality, but God condemns such things; therefore, we must condemn them also.

LOVE HAS PURE MOTIVES

Examine and test and evaluate your own selves to see whether you are holding to your faith and showing the proper fruits of it. . . .

—2 CORINTHIANS 13:5

Only God and we as individuals know our motives, and sometimes we don't even know them ourselves because we don't search our hearts to discover them. We can easily become accustomed to "doing," without realizing *why* we are doing what we are doing.

Over the years I have learned that God is very concerned with the "why behind the what." It is not actually what we do that impresses Him, but rather why we do it. People may be impressed with what we do, but God is not, unless our motives are pure.

For example, if I were to give a pastor a special seat in a conference to show him honor, that act would be acceptable to God. If I were to give him a preferred seat because I wanted to gain favor with him, God would not be pleased because my giving would not be done out of a motive of love (blessing one of God's servants), but a motive of selfishness (gaining something for myself).

First Corinthians 3:13-15 makes it very clear that we receive no reward for things done with impure motives:

The work of each [one] will become [plainly, openly] known (shown for what it is); for the day [of Christ] will disclose and declare it, because it will be revealed with fire, and the fire will test and critically appraise the character and worth of the work each person has done.

If the work which any person has built on this Foundation [any product of his efforts whatever] survives [this test], he will get his reward.

But if any person's work is burned up [under the test], he will suffer the loss [of it all, losing his reward], though he himself will be saved, but only as [one who has passed] through fire.

These Scriptures were made real to me by the Holy Spirit many years ago, and the principle they teach has helped me immensely in my walk with God and my dealings with other people.

If we, as believers, can develop a determination to live before God with pure motives, it will save us a lot of heartache and misery in life.

Jesus could read people's hearts. (John 2:24,25.) He always knew what was really in them, and that is no different today. We may succeed in fooling people, but not God.

Operating out of a pure heart also saves us a lot of time in life. I wasted a lot of years doing, doing, doing, and it seemed that most of what I did never succeeded. It took me a long time to realize that God will not bless actions done out of wrong motives. He will not answer prayers that are prayed with wrong motives:

. . . You do not have, because you do not ask.

[Or] you do ask [God for them] and yet fail to receive, because you ask with wrong purpose and evil, selfish motives. . . .

—JAMES 4:2,3

If we want our work to count for something and our prayers to be effective, we must learn to walk in love, which is not exclusive, unfriendly or inhospitable.

LOVE IS NOT "CLIQUISH"

Do not forget or neglect or refuse to extend hospitality to strangers [in the brotherhood – being friendly, cordial, and gracious, sharing the comforts of your home and doing your part generously], for through it some have entertained angels without knowing it.

—HEBREWS 13:2

A clique is an exclusive group, one to which not everyone is welcome. Being "in" makes us feel important, but being "out" can be very painful. I find that even the church is full of cliques.

A couple recently told me about being part of a cell group program in a certain church for a year and having to resign due to pressing family issues. They were leaving the church to go elsewhere because they felt that ever since they resigned their position, they were being treated differently. They said that while they once felt on the inside, now they felt on the outside. It seemed that people were not interested in associating with them now that they were no longer doing what the group was doing.

Naturally we have more to talk about with those who are doing the same things we are, but common decency requires us not to make others feel rejected because they are not part of our inner circle. We really need to develop more sensitivity to the feelings of others.

This couple did not quit the cell group because they wanted to; they did it because they felt it was God's direction for their family. If the people in that church had been truly "tuned in to the Holy Spirit," they would have realized that this couple felt left out and would have chosen to go out of their way to make them feel accepted.

If everyone in church on Sunday morning stands and greets others, and we notice an individual sitting in the pew who does not seem to know what to do, we should make sure that person feels welcome. When attending a party or group gathering, if everyone is talking and one individual is standing alone across the room, we should make a special effort to include that person in the group.

To be honest, sometimes this is work, and when we go to church for worship or go out for entertainment, who among us really wants to work? For many of us, talking to people we don't know is not comfortable. But building relationships *is* work; it requires effort.

As believers in the Lord Jesus Christ, you and I are instructed in the Word of God to make strangers feel welcome, to be hospitable toward them and not mistreat them in any way. This is especially important in church.

I wonder how many people finally get up enough courage to visit a church on Sunday morning but never go back because everyone there ignored them. Of course, not all churches are cold and uncaring; many are warm, friendly and loving, and those are the ones that will flourish. Everyone wants to be accepted, made to feel welcome and loved.

God gave the Israelites specific instructions not to wrong or oppress strangers, telling them to remember that they were once strangers in the land themselves. (Exodus 22:21.) We have all been the new person at work or at school, in a neighborhood or a church. We should remember how much we appreciated those who took the initiative to be friendly with us. We must always remember the golden rule: "Do unto others, as you would have them do unto you." (Luke 6:31.)

LOVE REACHES OUT TO ALL

So we are Christ's ambassadors, God making His appeal as it were through us. . . .
—2 CORINTHIANS 5:20

In the early days of my ministry on three separate occasions I singled out a particular lady in the church with whom I would like to become friends. In those days I was always looking for a "best friend." In each of these instances I felt I had found that friend. We did everything together. We had lunch together after my weekly meetings, shopped together, prayed together, talked on the phone, shared secrets, etc. I did not make a secret of the fact that each of those individuals was special in my life.

In all three relationships I ended up getting hurt and experiencing major rejection. As I sought God about why this kept happening to me, He showed me that I could not be a proper minister if I made one person in the church my special friend and much of the time excluded everyone else. He showed me how it made others feel, and asked me to think about how I would feel if someone was doing the same thing to me.

As we have seen, we certainly can have special friends, but we should not flaunt our friendships. We should not behave in such a way that the one friend is made to feel special while all the others are made to feel they are way down at the bottom of our list.

God showed me that He had to lift His anointing off of each of those three relationships of mine because I was showing partiality, and it was hurting other people. I wasn't hurting people on purpose; as a matter of fact, I really was not even aware that my attitude was wrong.

I am glad about what God taught me in those areas, but every once in a while I need a refresher course to keep me going in the right direction. I pray that the Lord will always let me know if my attitude or behavior is hurting other people.

God may choose and anoint you to be a very good friend to the pastor or the pastor's spouse, but it is wrong to use that friendship as a point of pride. Name-droppers get on my nerves. These are people who are constantly talking about every well-known individual they know personally. In my profession I frequently encounter such people, and they always make me feel uncomfortable.

As my ministry grew, and I was privileged to come into contact with many well-known people in ministry, I was frequently tempted to mention them in my sermons, but God quickly told me not to do so if my purpose was to impress others. It is sometimes very difficult to be that honest with ourselves, but it is the truth that makes us free.

Realizing that Jesus is a friend Who sticks closer than a brother (Proverbs 18:24), I finally decided to let Him be my best friend. Since then my relationships have been much more peaceful and less partial. I purposely do not allow myself to get into an unbalanced relationship with anyone.

Spending too much time with any one person or group of people is usually not good. We can appreciate each other more if everything stays in balance.

Proverbs 25:17 warns, *Let your foot seldom be in your neighbor's house, lest he become tired of you and hate you.*

Sometimes we learn so much about others that it makes it hard for us to love them. The more time we spend with people, the more likely we are to see their faults. The more we know of their personal life, the greater the temptation to judge things that are really none of our business.

We can keep ourselves from a great deal of trouble simply by striving for balance. It is unwise to become entangled in the affairs of anyone, especially a friend.

Jesus had many disciples, but He prayerfully chose twelve to have a closer walk with Him. Of those twelve, it appears He had even a closer relationship with three: Peter, James and John. He took them to the Mount of Transfiguration with Him and allowed them to go other places with Him that the rest of the twelve were not privileged to go.

Did Jesus love those three disciples more than all the others? The answer is definitely no! I believe that because He was aware of their destiny, He allowed them closer access to Him for their training and education. It is also possible those three loved Him more than the others. We always respond more to those people in our life who love us the most.

It is possible to be so advanced in our love walk that we love everybody equally, but there will always be those who receive and return our love more than others. Some individuals don't know how to receive love, and others only want to receive it without ever taking action to return it.

We should enlarge our circle of love. I long to see the day when love flows among believers like a mighty river. I believe at that time the world will sit up and take notice that God does indeed have something to offer them that they need.

We have previously seen in John 13:35 that Jesus said we would be recognized as His disciples by the love we have for one another. We must never forget that. We are His ambassadors, His representatives on this earth. As such, we must develop and exercise a strong love walk — with Him, with each other and with all those to whom He sends us. We must be channels through which flow His grace, His favor and His unchanging, unconditional, impartial love.

10

THE POISON OF PREJUDICE

There is [now no distinction] neither Jew nor Greek, there is neither slave nor free, there is not male and female; for you are all one in Christ Jesus.

—GALATIANS 3:28

As long as time has existed, Satan has breathed life into the poisonous practice of one race or group of people being prejudiced against another. Most wars are birthed out of prejudice and hatred. The Holocaust came from the same poison, and so did slavery.

Cain hated Abel (Genesis 4:2-8), and it seems hatred has never stopped. Hating people is hard work, and it kills everything good in life. Even various religious sects have hated one another and allowed the spirit of pride to fill their hearts.

You and I may not agree with everything another person believes or does, but we have no right to hate him because of it, and we certainly should not mistreat him.

God hates sin, but He loves every sinner. He hates stubbornness and rebellion, but still loves the person who is stubborn and rebellious. He has not told us we have to approve of everyone's beliefs, choices and actions, but He has told us to love everyone.

There are so many denominations and independent churches it is almost unbelievable, and yet there is only one Bible. It is evident that God has one thing to say to all people, one plan for our conduct and relationship with Him; but we have developed many churches and church groups to suit our own varying ways of interpreting what the Bible says.

I have finally come to realize that probably none of us are 100 percent correct. Most of the things we fight about are petty things anyway.

Jesus told the Pharisees that they strained at a gnat and swallowed a camel. (Matthew 23:24 KJV.) They had gotten so picky about little things that really did not make any difference, it prevented them from centering in on the main things that were truly vital.

Paul dealt with the same divisive attitudes in the early church.

IS CHRIST DIVIDED?

For it has been made clear to me, my brethren, by those of Chloe's household, that there are contentions and wrangling and factions among you.

What I mean is this, that each one of you [either]
says, I belong to Paul, or I belong to Apollos, or I
belong to Cephas (Peter), or I belong to Christ.

Is Christ (the Messiah) divided into parts? Was Paul
crucified on behalf of you? Or were you baptized into
the name of Paul?

—1 CORINTHIANS 1:11-13

Christ is not divided into parts, and neither can His body be divided. In Matthew 12:25 He warned: . . . *Any kingdom that is divided against itself is being brought to desolation and laid waste, and no city or house divided against itself will last or continue to stand.*

As members of the church, the body of Christ, we are power-less as long as we are filled with prejudice, hatred and disharmony. Agreement brings power. Satan knows this very well and fights it with every ounce of strength he possesses. (Ephesians 6:12.) We must not allow him to win the war. We can defeat him with love, but we play right into his hands through anything that contributes to division.

How can we expect the world ever to be at peace, if we Christians cannot be at peace? Our love walk must be examined and looked at through the eyes of Jesus and any necessary changes made.

I experienced some of the most severe rejection in my life from Christians who did not agree with certain decisions I felt God was leading me to make. It is amazing how people reject us if we do not agree with them and follow the same path they have taken. I think we can surely learn to disagree agreeably and even respect each other's right to have personal opinions.

I don't mind people disagreeing with me if they do it respect-fully, still honoring me as a person. I may not always be right, but I do have a right to do what I truly believe God is leading me to do. I even have a right to make my own mistakes. Sometimes that is the only way to learn what is truly right.

We must avoid being prejudiced toward people because they are not like us, because they are of a different color, religion, sex or culture.

WHAT COLOR IS LOVE?

> . . . For the Lord sees not as man sees; for man looks on the outward appearance, but the Lord looks on the heart.
>
> —1 SAMUEL 16:7

I love the title of Creflo A. Dollar Jr.'s popular book, *The Color of Love*.[1] What color do we think love is? Is it white? Is it black? Perhaps it is red or yellow or even brown. We all know better than that. God is love, and He has no color.

As I travel the world, I am continually amazed at the differ-ences in people. Each culture has a wide variety of things that are different from my own. Often I don't like the food in different places, but that does not mean the food is bad; it just means I don't like it. In some areas the people are gentle, and in others they are more harsh; some are warm and friendly, while others are cold and unfriendly.

I was recently in a country where I noticed if I smiled at people, their faces remained hard and suspicious. I learned they had been under Soviet domination for fifty years and had endured great persecution and evil treatment during Stalin's rule. Love caused me to pray for those people and to continue trying to find ways to break down the walls of hatred and suspicion that had been built up during those decades of pain. I am so glad that God did not try only one time to be friendly with me, but that He kept trying until He found a way to reach me.

Recently I read an article in *Guideposts* magazine about a woman who lived next door to an elderly lady who never came out of her house or even lifted her window shades to let in any light.[2] This lady's husband had died, and she herself had endured a stroke, which had left her lonely and bitter.

The woman and her two young children began trying to reach out to the elderly recluse, but each time their advances were totally rejected. They baked cookies every week for a long time and delivered them to their neighbor's door. The first time they brought her cookies, she opened the door just a crack, accepted the cookies, thanked them and closed the door.

The neighbor's unfavorable response was not what the Christian woman hoped for, but the determination to see if love would really work gave her the zeal to keep on keeping on.

Eventually love did work. The elderly lady accepted a casserole from her and said more than just a thank you. As the visits continued, the elderly woman gradually began to chat longer.

Finally one day the Christian woman's children picked some flowers from her garden and delivered them to her neighbor, and eventually they became good friends. The elderly lady got her life back. She opened her blinds, her door and her heart and began to live again.

FORGIVENESS PRODUCES
A DOUBLE BLESSING

Instead of your [former] shame you shall have a twofold recompense; instead of dishonor and reproach [your people] shall rejoice in their portion. Therefore in their land they shall possess double [what they had forfeited]; everlasting joy shall be theirs.

For I the Lord love justice. . . .

—Isaiah 61:7,8

Are you prejudiced against anyone for any reason? If so, that prejudice needs to be totally eradicated from your mind and attitude.

You may be thinking, "Well, Joyce, that is easy for you to say. You were not the one hurt by this individual or group."

That is true, but I have been hurt in life to a very deep degree. I was abused, abandoned, rejected, blamed, lied about, misunderstood and betrayed by family and friends. I was abused sexually, verbally, emotionally and mentally, and I allowed Satan to fill my heart with hatred for those who hurt me. But when I began to learn about love, I moved from hatred to bitterness, then to mild resentment and finally to freedom, which comes only through forgiveness.

When we forgive an injustice, we are actually doing ourselves a favor; we are giving ourselves a gift of freedom.

God promises to bring justice into our lives and to give us a double reward for our former shame, pain and unfair treatment. When we try to bring justice ourselves through vengeful acts intended to hurt those who hurt us, we only tie God's hands and prevent Him from working in our behalf.

If you have been hurt, God knows all about it, and He has a plan for your vindication. As we saw in Chapter 7, He is the Vindicator. (Hebrews 10:30.)

The Lord gloriously brought restitution into my life, and in ways that only He could have done. He took what Satan meant for harm and worked it for good. (See Romans 8:28.)

The absolute key to unlocking the recompense of God for past hurts, however, is to do things His way and not our own. As stated earlier, in His Word, He tells us plainly how to handle our enemies: We are to love them, pray for them and bless them.

Love includes forgiveness, and forgiveness requires letting go of the past. It is impossible to forgive and forget while still harboring resentment and hostility. Fresh water and bitter water cannot come out of the same fountain (James 3:11). That kind of mixture poisons everything.

CHRIST HAS BROKEN DOWN
THE DIVIDING WALL

> For He is [Himself] our peace (our bond of unity and harmony). He has made us both [Jew and Gentile] one [body], and has broken down (destroyed, abolished) the hostile dividing wall between us.
> —EPHESIANS 2:14

Jesus dealt with dividing walls in His day. The Jews felt contempt for the Gentiles, whom they called dogs.[3] Many men saw women as inferior and, as a result of their wrong attitude, sometimes women were mistreated.[4]

As a woman I could look back and decide to hate all men because my female ancestors were treated unfairly. In the same way, Jews could spend their lives hating Germans because of a crazy, demon-possessed man named Adolf Hitler. Americans could hate the Japanese because they bombed Pearl Harbor and thrust the United States into World War II. African-Americans could spend their lives hating white people because of slavery.

Actually the list could be endless if we went back to the beginning of time. The problems we have in our society today are not new; they are just compounding because they have been around so long.

None of us can go back and undo the past. No matter how much we would like to, it is not possible. We cannot even pay people back for what they did to us or failed to do for us in the past. Only God can do that. Our only peaceful option is to forget what lies behind and press on to what lies ahead. (Philippians 3:13,14.)

In my own life I finally had to stop taking an inventory of what I had lost and begin to count up what I had left. In the beginning it did not seem like very much, but I made the choice to give it to God. It is amazing what God can do with a few fragments. He has more than paid me back for the hurt and pain in my past and has given me a wonderful life that is bearing good fruit.

How sad it would have been if I had spent my life in bitterness, hating all men because some men had abused me, or hating all my family members because some of them had rejected me, or hating all church people because some had betrayed me.

Life is too short to spend it hating.

Examine yourself in this area. Be honest with yourself concerning whether or not you are prejudiced. Even if you find only a little bit of prejudice, repent of it and pray sincerely that it will be removed from your heart. Say to yourself, "I am no better than anyone else; we are all equal in God's eyes. Every person is God's creation, and He stated that everything He made was good."

Remember, our enemy is not people; it is not flesh and blood who may cause us some temporary pain and discomfort. Our enemy is Satan who is out to totally destroy us. (Ephesians 6:12.) We must not waste our time and energy hating each other and fighting against each other, but rather walking in love to wage spiritual warfare against our real enemy. Love is one of the highest forms of spiritual warfare we can do.

11

LOVE IS SPIRITUAL WARFARE

*For we are not wrestling with flesh and blood
[contending only with physical opponents], but
against the despotisms, against the powers, against
[the master spirits who are] the world rulers of this
present darkness, against the spirit forces of wickedness in the heavenly (supernatural) sphere.*

—Ephesians 6:12

When I first became aware of the fact that I had an enemy,
Satan, who wanted to kill, steal and destroy everything good God
had planned for me (John 10:10), I was very interested in learning
how to defeat him. Teaching on spiritual warfare was very popular
at that time, and I attended many sessions on the subject. Desiring
to learn all I could, I also listened to teaching tapes and read books.

In the course of my studies, I learned many interesting, biblical principles and began attempting to exercise my authority as a
believer. I rebuked evil spirits, cast them out, bound them and

loosed the Holy Ghost. I fasted, resisted, stood firm and did see some progress, but to say I was walking in the power that the Word of God said was available to me would be a definite overstatement. I wanted to live in the reality of Scriptures like these spoken by Jesus to His disciples:

> Behold! I have given you authority and power to trample upon serpents and scorpions, and [physical and mental strength and ability] over all the power that the enemy [possesses]; and nothing shall in any way harm you.
>
> —LUKE 10:19

> I will give you the keys of the kingdom of heaven; and whatever you bind (declare to be improper and unlawful) on earth must be what is already bound in heaven; and whatever you loose (declare lawful) on earth must be what is already loosed in heaven.
>
> —MATTHEW 16:19

> And these attesting signs will accompany those who believe: in My name they will drive out demons. . . .
>
> —MARK 16:17

I finally realized I had developed many methods and was doing a lot of shouting, but that the real power I sought was missing.

About that same time the Holy Spirit began to teach me many things about love. I began to see that a lot of my problems resulted from the fact that I had not developed a strong love walk. I also began to get a revelation that no matter how many methods of warfare I knew, they were empty exercises unless the real power of God was flowing through them. It was like having a gun but no bullets, or a bow without any arrows.

I was trying to defeat Satan without ammunition!

As we have seen, Galatians 5:6 teaches us that faith works and is energized (activated and expressed) by love. I thought I was a great woman of faith, but obviously according to this Scripture, my faith was not energized and working because I was not walking in love.

I came to see that knowing that God loved me would energize me (move me) to lean on Him and place my faith in Him, and that learning to walk in love with others would give me the power I needed to defeat Satan.

One day as I was screaming at demons, doing what I thought was spiritual warfare, the Father spoke to my heart and said, "Joyce, why don't you look in the Bible and examine how Jesus waged spiritual warfare?"

When I did so, it became obvious to me that Satan had no power over Him. Why was that? What did Jesus do that I was missing? What did He have that I didn't have?

THE WARFARE OF PEACE

Therefore take up the whole armor of God, that you may be able to withstand in the evil day, and having done all, to stand.

Stand therefore, having girded your waist with truth, having put on the breastplate of righteousness,

And having shod your feet with the preparation of the gospel of peace.

—EPHESIANS 6:13-15 NKJV

As I continued to study the Bible, I learned some life-changing things. One of the things I learned about was the warfare of rest. Jesus always walked in peace. Even in the midst of storms He remained peaceful. (Mark 4:35-39; John 6:16-20)

In Ephesians 6, which describes the armor of God, I noticed verse 15 NKJV says . . . *having shod your feet with the preparation of the gospel of peace.* That speaks of what could be called "shoes of peace." Shoes help us to walk and not get injured. "Shoes of peace" have been given to every believer as part of our spiritual armor to help us walk in the Spirit and not get injured in our inner man. But not all of us are wearing our armor. Many of us are carrying it around with us, but we're not putting it on.

Ephesians 6:11 tells us: *Put on God's whole armor [the armor of a heavy-armed soldier which God supplies], that you may be able successfully to stand up against [all] the strategies and the deceits of the devil.* As I studied that passage, I saw that I was instructed to "put on" the full armor of God so that I might be able to defeat the enemy.

I have never walked into my closet and had my clothes or shoes jump on my body. I have always had to put them on. So we must "put on" the armor of God, including the "shoes of peace." To me that means we must walk in peace on purpose; we cannot wait for peace to fall on us.

A decision to be a peacemaker takes a serious commitment and a lot of humility. I know because there are times when I simply want to lose my temper about something, throw a fit and tell someone off. There was a time in my life when that is exactly what I did. I have learned it does me very little good. Oh, I may get to blow off a little steam, which may make me feel better for a while, but it is like getting drunk and then having a hangover.

I found that being upset always left me with a "hangover." I usually had a headache, I lost my joy, I was filled with wrong thoughts — in general, I felt "yucky." I also discovered that once I allowed myself to get really upset, it took a long time to completely get over it — mentally and emotionally as well as physically. The short-term fleshly "kick" I got out of doing it my way really was not worth it.

If we stay in peace and trust God, He will defeat our enemies: *And do not [for a moment] be frightened or intimidated in anything by your opponents and adversaries, for such [constancy and fearlessness] will be a clear sign (proof and seal) to them of [their impending] destruction, but [a sure token and evidence] of your deliverance and salvation, and that from God* (Philippians 1:28).

Always remember: *No peace = no power. Know peace = know power.*

GOD'S PRESENCE OR HIS PRESENTS?

You will show me the path of life; in Your presence is fullness of joy, at Your right hand there are pleasures forevermore.

—Psalm 16:11

Another thing I learned as I studied the Bible was to seek God's face and not just His hand.

Seeking God for Who He is, not just for what He can do for us, is vital to our victory as believers. If we will seek Him, His Word promises us that He will protect us: *He who dwells in the secret place of the Most High shall remain stable and fixed under the shadow of the Almighty [Whose power no foe can withstand]* (Psalm 91:1).

The psalmist David had learned this same lesson, as we can see from the following Scripture:

> *One thing have I asked of the Lord, that will I seek, inquire for, and [insistently] require: that I may dwell in the house of the Lord [in His presence] all the days of my life, to behold and gaze upon the beauty [the sweet attractiveness and the delightful loveliness] of the Lord and to meditate, consider, and inquire in His temple.*
>
> *For in the day of trouble He will hide me in His shelter; in the secret place of His tent will He hide me; He will set me high upon a rock.*
>
> *And now shall my head be lifted up above my enemies round about me. . . .*
>
> —PSALM 27:4-6

This was a major lesson for me. I had to learn to rejoice in God, not in what He was doing or not doing for me. The joy of the Lord is our strength (Nehemiah 8:10), not the joy of circumstances.

We will have little or no strength against the devil if we are unstable and allow our circumstances to determine our joy.

It took a while for me to make this transition, but what an awesome difference it made in my spiritual life. Previously, I had always felt that I needed something, that something was missing in my walk with the Lord. I found it all in His Presence, not in His presents.

What we are looking for is not God's gifts, but God Himself. His Presence is what sustains us and gives us life — abundant and everlasting life.

In John 6 the Jews had seen Jesus miraculously feed 5,000 people with only five loaves of bread and two fishes. But in verse 30 they had asked Him for more evidence that He was really sent from God. Jesus told them, *Your forefathers ate the manna in the wilderness, and [yet] they died* (v. 49). Then in verse 51 He said, *I [Myself] am this Living Bread that came down from heaven. If anyone eats of this Bread, he will live forever.* . . . Later in the same chapter He said, *. . . whoever continues to feed on Me [whoever takes Me for his food and is nourished by Me] shall [in his turn] live through and because of Me* (v. 57).

In this passage, Jesus said that He was living bread and living drink and that anyone who ate and drank of Him would never hunger and never thirst. He was, of course, speaking of spiritual hunger and thirst (the void people feel when they don't spend enough time in God's Presence and with His Word). Material things cannot satisfy a hungry soul. Only God can truly satisfy any individual.

The Lord was doing a lot of things for me, and I was seeing many miracles in my life, yet I was still dissatisfied. It was time for transition. God had established a relationship with me by doing things for me. Now it was time for me to prove my love for Him by seeking to do His will, not just seeking Him for what He could do for me.

I was like the Israelites who had been eating manna every day. I was enjoying God's provision, but I had not learned simply to enjoy His Presence.

A thorough study of John 6 reveals that when Jesus presented to His disciples and followers this message about eating His flesh and drinking His blood, many of them said it was offensive and hard to bear: *After this, many of His disciples drew back (returned to their old associations) and no longer accompanied Him* (v. 66).

I believe many people are willing to follow Jesus if He is taking them where they want to go and doing for them what they want done. But when it comes time for this very needful transition in their relationship with Him, many cannot make the turn. Their carnal desires get the upper hand, and they backslide.

We must decide that we will serve God even if we never get what we want. Like Job, we must say, *Though he slay me, yet will I trust in him . . .* (Job 13:15 KJV).

God has actually done more for me since the time I totally surrendered my will to His than He had ever done previously. However, I did go through a time of testing in which I had to seek Him simply for Himself and not for anything He might give me.

The Lord actually challenged me not to ask Him for one earthly thing again until He told me I could do so. Each time I would begin to pray for some material thing, it was as though I had fish bones in my throat so that I had to stop and change my prayer. This lasted for about six months. Then one day God told me to pray for something specific that I had been desiring, and I was almost afraid to do it.

I had come into such a wonderful sense of peace and joy from learning to enjoy His Presence instead of His presents that I did not want to go back to where I had come from spiritually. The Lord assured me that a work had been done in me and that I would not go back to my old ways. He was correct.

Since that time my prayer life has been different. It is no longer filled with petition. I do ask God for things I desire, but I spend much more time praising and thanking Him, loving and adoring Him, sitting in His Presence and enjoying Him, than I ever do making personal requests. He knows the desires of my heart, and as I delight myself in Him, He gives them to me, just as He has promised in His Word. (Psalm 37:4.)

THE WARFARE OF OBEDIENCE

> *So Jesus answered them by saying, I assure you, most solemnly I tell you, the Son is able to do nothing of Himself (of His own accord); but He is able to do only what He sees the Father doing, for whatever the Father does is what the Son does in the same way [in His turn].*
>
> —JOHN 5:19

From my study I came to realize that Jesus had power over Satan because He was always obedient to the Father. He actually said that He neither said nor did anything that He did not first see the Father do. (John 8:28,29.) None of us are at that level yet, but it should certainly be our goal.

In the current church age, we need more teaching on obedience and holiness (moral goodness).[1] There is a great deal of teaching on faith, prosperity and success, all of which are very important. I am very thankful that someone taught me I could prosper. But God is not going to give a bunch of spiritual babies radical prosperity that would only serve to make them more carnal.

As Jesus told us, we should concentrate on seeking spiritual maturity, and God will see to our material blessings: . . . *seek ye first the kingdom of God, and his righteousness; and all these things shall be added unto you* (Matthew 6:33 KJV).

For years I had heard one-half of James 4:7 KJV quoted: . . . *Resist the devil, and he will flee from you.* It can be very misleading to quote only half of a Scripture or to read it out of context. This Scripture actually says, *Submit yourselves therefore to God. Resist the devil, and he will flee from you.*

That tells me if I will submit myself to God (obey what He tells me to do) first, then I will be able to resist the devil, and he will flee from me.

During the time that God was teaching me what true spiritual warfare was, I will admit that I was not as concerned about obedience as I should have been. I wanted my problems to go away. I thought Satan was my problem, and I wanted power over him. I didn't realize that power over the devil comes only from an obedient lifestyle. (Matthew 17:21.)

Once again I made a transition. I began to major in what God said was really important, and as I did, I began to see major differences in my life and circumstances. Not all my problems went away, and Satan did not stop attacking me altogether, but concentrating on what God wanted me to do instead of on how to get rid of the enemy made my problems seem smaller.

Whatever we concentrate on in our life is the thing that will seem biggest to us. We need to magnify the Lord (Psalm 34:3,4), not what the enemy is doing.

THE WARFARE OF WORDS

I will not talk with you much more, for the prince (evil genius, ruler) of the world is coming. And he has no claim on Me. [He has nothing in common with Me; there is nothing in Me that belongs to him, and he has no power over Me.]

But [Satan is coming and] I do as the Father has commanded Me, so that the world may know (be convinced) that I love the Father and that I do only what the Father has instructed Me to do. [I act in full agreement with His orders.]. . . .

—JOHN 14:30,31

Next the Holy Spirit taught me the importance of words and how we often open doors for the enemy with our words.

Jesus was very careful about what He said. In the Old Testament, Isaiah prophesied of Him: *He was oppressed, [yet when] He was afflicted, He was submissive and opened not His mouth . . .* (Isaiah 53:7). In John 14:30, Jesus told His disciples that He would not be talking with them much more, because the time had come for Him to do what His Father had sent Him to do. He knew it would be an intense time of great pressure. I believe He said this to His disciples because He knew something most of us still need to learn:

Talking too much when we are under pressure usually causes us to say something we are sorry for later.

Jesus knew the importance of words. He had come too far to open a door for Satan now.

So often we pray and ask God for help, and then when we feel pressured, we say something that negates our prayer. God cannot help us if we don't get in agreement with His Word and stay in agreement with it. We must hold fast our confession of faith in Him. (Hebrews 10:23 NKJV.)

This does not mean that we are to refuse to face reality or to ignore or lie about our circumstances, but it does mean that we are to stay positive in the midst of those circumstances.

We can share with others what is going on in our lives; we all need others to help us through the hard times. But to talk about our problems incessantly doesn't do anybody any good. Often it makes our problems seem larger than they really are, and it wears out our friends until they don't want to spend time with us any longer.

If we are gossiping about other people, saying unkind and unloving things about them, we will not be successful when we have a problem and try to exercise faith to take authority over Satan. We must remember that love covers a multitude of sins; it does not expose the faults of others. Gossiping, backbiting and talebearing are major problems for those who want to exercise spiritual authority, as are complaining, murmuring and faultfinding.

We need to use our mouths for what God gave them to us for and stop opening doors for Satan with wrong words.

Start being more careful about what you say, and you will find that you have more authority over the devil.

Learning to keep my word was another big breakthrough for me. Integrity and honor do not seem to be important in our society today, but they are very important to God. He wants us to realize that even as we expect Him to keep His Word to us, He expects us to keep our word to Him and to others.

It is very easy in a moment of emotions to say what we will do, but the doing of it is the real test of character. We should be adamant about keeping our word. We may forget what we tell people we will do, but they don't forget, and neither does the Lord.

Being people of integrity gives us power over our enemies:

> *The Lord judges the people; judge me, O Lord, and do me justice according to my righteousness [my rightness, justice, and right standing with You] and according to the integrity that is in me.*
>
> *Oh, let the wickedness of the wicked come to an end, but establish the [uncompromisingly] righteous [those upright and in harmony with You]. . . .*
>
> —PSALM 7:8,9

> *By this I know that You favor and delight in me, because my enemy does not triumph over me.*

And as for me, You have upheld me in my integrity
and set me in Your presence forever.

—PSALM 41:11,12

David sought to be a man of integrity. He knew it gave him power with God and that God would give him power over his enemies.

The same set of rules applies to everyone. God has precepts that we must live by if we intend to enjoy the type of life Jesus died to give us. Multitudes live far below the level their heavenly Father intended, and it is not the fault of their past, their circumstances or the devil. It is because they are making wrong choices.

Satan may be at the root of our problems, but he always leads us into some kind of disobedience or deception that creates the real problem. Trying to get rid of Satan without getting rid of the behavior pattern that is causing the problem is foolish and a waste of time.

By all means, we should exercise our authority as believers. God created Adam and Eve and told them to subdue the earth and exercise dominion over it. (Genesis 1:27,28.) They were to rule — not Satan, not their circumstances nor anything else. They were to stay under God's leadership and then rule in His behalf, bringing His will to pass on earth. That is still God's plan for mankind.

Resist the devil in Jesus' name. Be aggressive against him: *Withstand him; be firm in faith [against his onset – rooted, established, strong, immovable, and determined]* . . . (1 Peter 5:9). Don't believe his lies. Walk in your authority. But don't make the mistake that I did, thinking I could operate in methods of spiritual warfare without living the lifestyle I needed to empower the methods.

THE WARFARE OF LOVE

Above all things have intense and unfailing love for one another, for love covers a multitude of sins [forgives and disregards the offenses of others].
—1 PETER 4:8

One of the most amazing things I learned, one that still thrills my soul, is that love is actually spiritual warfare. This truth makes spiritual warfare fun, because loving people is very enjoyable.

I learned that instead of looking like I am "oppressed and under something" all the time, I can actually look happy. I have found that I can be on the attack instead of under the attack.

First Peter 4:8 teaches us to have intense love for one another. The *King James Version* uses the word "fervent." The verb form of the Greek word translated *fervent* means "to be hot, to boil."[2] Our love walk needs to be hot, on fire, boiling over, not cold and barely noticeable.

I heard someone say that even a fly is smart enough not to light on a hot stove. If we are hot enough with love, Satan won't be able to handle us. We might say we will be "too hot to handle."

Have you ever microwaved something for too long and couldn't get it out of the oven because it was too hot to handle? That's the way I want to be. I want Satan to dread seeing me get out of bed in the morning.

That's the way our love should be -- hot, not cold.

COLD LOVE: A SIGN OF THE END TIMES

And the love of the great body of people will grow cold because of the multiplied lawlessness and iniquity,

But he who endures to the end will be saved.

—MATTHEW 24:12,13

The twenty-fourth chapter of Matthew deals with signs of the end times. Most of them we are very familiar with — wars and rumors of wars, earthquakes, famines and widespread deception. But another sign of the end times is found in that chapter, one I had never heard anyone mention. Verse 12 says the love of the great body of people will grow cold due to the lawlessness and wickedness in the land.

As I pondered that Scripture I began to realize that the great body is the church, not the world. I saw that all the pressure of rampant evil, trying circumstances and even the stress of our lifestyle in the modern world was indeed producing an atmosphere so supercharged with problems that most people were totally ignoring their love walk and concentrating on looking out for themselves and solving their own problems.

This is something that God never told us to do. If we tend to His business, He will tend to ours. We are to concentrate on representing Him properly, which is impossible unless we are walking in love. As we do that, He will give us wisdom to deal with our stresses and deliverance from our foes.

God does not always give us the ability to solve our own problems, yet when we are powerless to solve our own, He does enable us to solve someone else's.

In my own life, I realized I was spinning my wheels, so to speak. I was trying to solve all my problems, thinking when my life got straightened out, then I could go forward in ministry to others. The fact is, I had it backwards, and so do many others.

I needed to cast my care on the Lord, do what He showed me to do concerning my situations in life, but not get entangled in them. I needed to sow seeds in someone else's life by helping them, and then God would bring a harvest in my own life.

We should march against Satan with *love.*

Refuse to let your love grow cold. Stir up the love in your marriage, toward your family and friends. Reach out to others who are in need and hurting. Pray for people, bless them. Grow to the point that early in the morning your heart is filled with thoughts of how you can bless someone that day.

DON'T LET SELFISHNESS WIN THE WAR

For though we walk (live) in the flesh, we are not carrying on our warfare according to the flesh and using mere human weapons.

For the weapons of our warfare are not physical [weapons of flesh and blood], but they are mighty before God for the overthrow and destruction of strongholds,

[Inasmuch as we] refute arguments and theories and reasonings and every proud and lofty thing that sets itself up against the [true] knowledge of God; and we lead every thought and purpose away captive into the obedience of Christ (the Messiah, the Anointed One).
—2 CORINTHIANS 10:3-5

We are definitely in a war. The Bible teaches us that the weapons of our warfare are not carnal, natural weapons, but ones that are mighty through God for the pulling down of strongholds. The stronghold of cold love must be pulled down in our lives.

The *King James Version* of verse 5 speaks of casting down imaginations, and every high thing that exalts itself against the knowledge of God. "Casting down" wrong thinking is vital to proper spiritual warfare. Selfish, self-centered, "what about me?" thinking is definitely wrong thinking.

Galatians 6:10 says we should be mindful (have our minds full) of ways we can be a blessing to others. I regret to say we are prone to having our minds on ourselves more than on anything else.

I believe Satan has launched high-tech spiritual warfare against the church, using humanism, materialism and widespread selfishness as his bait. We must win the war against these things, and the only way to combat them is with a strong love walk. We must remember that the way we overcome evil is with good. (Romans 12:21.)

Purposely forgetting about ourselves and our problems and doing something for someone else while we are hurting is one of the most powerful things we can do to overcome evil.

When Jesus was on the cross in intense suffering, He took time to comfort the thief next to Him. (Luke 23:39-43.)

When Stephen was being stoned, he prayed for those stoning him, asking God not to lay the sin to their charge. (Acts 7:59,60.)

When Paul and Silas were in prison, they took time to minister to their jailer. Even after God came on the scene and suddenly a powerful earthquake hit that broke their chains and opened the door for them to come out, they remained just for the purpose of ministering to their captor. How tempting it must have been to run away quickly while the opportunity was there, how tempting to take care of themselves and not worry about anyone else. Their act of love moved the man to ask how he might be saved, and he and his entire family were born again (asked Jesus into their hearts). (Acts 16:25-34.)

I believe if we as the church of Jesus Christ, His body here on earth, will wage war against selfishness and walk in love, the world will begin to take notice. We will not impress the world by being just like them. But how many unsaved friends and relatives might come to know Jesus if we genuinely loved them instead of ignoring, judging or rejecting them? I believe it is time to find out, don't you?

12

SERVING GOD IS
SERVING ONE ANOTHER

*Whatever may be your task, work at it heartily (from
the soul), as [something done] for the Lord and not
for men,*

*Knowing [with all certainty] that it is from the Lord
[and not from men] that you will receive the inheritance
which is your [real] reward. [The One Whom] you are
actually serving [is] the Lord Christ (the Messiah).*

—COLOSSIANS 3:23,24

One morning as I got up and went downstairs to make coffee,
I felt the Lord tug at my heart to make Dave a fruit salad. Our
housekeeper was off that day, and Dave really enjoyed his fruit
salad in the morning. To be honest, I did not want to make a fruit
salad. I could have handled bringing Dave an apple and a banana,
but I did not want to take the time to cut them all up in a bowl and
serve it to him. I wanted to go pray and read my Bible!

Sometimes we make the mistake of thinking that spiritual activity replaces obedience and makes us spiritual, but it doesn't.

The Lord spoke to my heart that serving Dave was actually serving Him. I obediently made the fruit salad.

I wonder how many marriages could have been saved from the divorce courts had the partners been willing to serve one another through love. It seems that everyone today wants to be free, and Jesus has indeed set us free, but He has not set us free to be selfish and to want to be served, but rather to serve others.

FREE TO BE SERVANTS

For you, brethren, were [indeed] called to freedom; only [do not let your] freedom be an incentive to your flesh and an opportunity or excuse [for selfishness], but through love you should serve one another.

For the whole Law [concerning human relationships] is complied with in the one precept, You shall love your neighbor as [you do] yourself.

—GALATIANS 5:13,14

I definitely love my husband, but the fulfillment of love must find some service to flow through.

Jesus said, in essence, "If you love Me, you will obey Me." (John 14:21.) To say "I love Jesus" and walk in disobedience is deception. Words are wonderful, but a full love walk must be much more than words.

How can I say I love my husband if I never want to do anything for him? It is very easy to slide into the worldly flow of "everybody wait on me," but I am determined to swim upstream, against the pull of my flesh, and to be a servant and a blessing everywhere I go.

We must not forget what Jesus said in Matthew 25:34-45:

> *Then the King will say to those at His right hand, Come, you blessed of My Father [you favored of God and appointed to eternal salvation], inherit (receive as your own) the kingdom prepared for you from the foundation of the world.*
>
> *For I was hungry and you gave Me food, I was thirsty and you gave Me something to drink, I was a stranger and you brought Me together with yourselves and welcomed and entertained and lodged Me.*
>
> *I was naked and you clothed Me, I was sick and you visited Me with help and ministering care, I was in prison and you came to see Me.*
>
> *Then the just and upright will answer Him, Lord, when did we see You hungry and gave You food, or thirsty and gave You something to drink?*
>
> *And when did we see You a stranger and welcomed and entertained You, or naked and clothed You?*
>
> *And when did we see You sick or in prison and came to visit You?*

And the King will reply to them, Truly I tell you, in so far as you did it for one of the least [in the estimation of men] of these My brethren, you did it for Me.

Then He will say to those at His left hand, Begone from Me, you cursed, into the eternal fire prepared for the devil and his angels!

For I was hungry and you gave Me no food, I was thirsty and you gave Me nothing to drink,

I was a stranger and you did not welcome Me and entertain Me, I was naked and you did not clothe Me, I was sick and in prison and you did not visit Me with help and ministering care.

Then they also [in their turn] will answer, Lord, when did we see You hungry or thirsty or a stranger or naked or sick or in prison, and did not minister to You?

And He will reply to them, Solemnly I declare to you, in so far as you failed to do it for the least [in the estimation of men] of these, you failed to do it for Me.

In this passage Jesus makes it plain enough. If we have done nothing kind for others, then we have done nothing for Him.

When we serve one another, the One we are actually serving is Christ, and we should know that our reward will come from Him.

I don't recall getting any particular reward that morning for making Dave's fruit salad. He did thank me, but nothing spectacular occurred as a result of the act of kindness. However, I am sure that God rewarded me that day with peace and joy and a sense of

His manifest Presence. I am also sure that He arranged for someone else to do something for me, something that person would not have done had I not sown that seed of obedience.

We lose a lot of blessings we never even know about simply because we fail to do for others what we would like done for us. We always look to get blessed in return from the people we bless, but it does not always work that way. We should do what we do unto the Lord and look to Him for our reward. Sometimes God will actually prevent others from doing what we would like them to do for us, because we have our eyes too much on them and not enough on Him.

My husband is very good to me; he does many lovely things for me, and I make an effort to be kind and good to him.

A marriage does not stay good just because it started good. It does not stay exciting unless it is kept exciting. All food is bland without some spice, and many people have very bland marriages because they fail to add the spice of doing nice things for one another.

If your marriage is not what you would like it to be, you could literally turn it around by adopting this one principle I am sharing right now. You may have been waiting for your marriage partner to do something for you, and perhaps you have even been stubbornly refusing to be the first to make a move. Swallow your pride and save your marriage. Begin to serve your marriage partner and see it as serving Christ. Do the things you know your mate enjoys, get dressed up for him or her, look your best, smile, stop being a nag or a complainer. Buy your spouse little gifts, leave love notes, have fun together. Work at your marriage because if you don't work at making it good, Satan will definitely work at making it fail.

Try the same thing with your friends and other family members. Little things can make a big difference in relationships.

Many people never seem to have the marriage they have always dreamed of. That can be changed, but it requires time and effort. If you will take that time and make that effort, you won't be disappointed.

GREATNESS THROUGH SERVICE

> . . . *whoever desires to be great among you must be your servant,*
>
> *And whoever wishes to be most important and first in rank among you must be slave of all.*
>
> *For even the Son of Man came not to have service rendered to Him, but to serve. . . .*
>
> —MARK 10:43-45

A servant is one who lives to benefit another, one who sacrifices for another's joy or fulfillment. Sacrifice is the only status symbol in the kingdom of God. Jesus said servanthood makes a person great, and that no one can become great without it.

I once released a powerful series of teaching tapes on servanthood titled "What Makes a Great Man Great?" I was disappointed to find that it was not selling very well. I believe the reason is that we are often like children who don't want to eat our vegetables. We like the things that taste good, but often ignore the things we really need to be healthy.

At one time in my life I would not touch vegetables. As a child I had not been taught to like them, so I stayed away from them. I liked pasta, fried foods, cakes and pies, potatoes and meat. As a result I was overweight and felt bad.

Later, I learned to like fruits and vegetables and other foods that were better for me. Now I actually crave vegetables. If I go very long without eating generous portions of them, I really miss them.

I am finally becoming the same way about walking in love and serving others. I often tell my children, "You'd better hang out with me today, because I'm having a giving attack." They know that means I am going to bless whoever is in my way, and if they are smart, they will stick close to me and get blessed.

I was so very selfish for so many years; I am grateful God in His mercy is helping me see the importance of being reduced to love. There is nothing in the world that is more important. The Lord has done something in my heart, something He has been working on for almost twelve years as of this writing.

I remember when He initially began dealing with me about my love walk. I can tell you it has been a long, sometimes hard and yet wonderful journey. It has freed me from myself.

I was imprisoned in my own little narrow world, always trying to take care of me. What a completely awesome delight it is to actually wake up in the morning and find God and others on my mind first. I want to obey Galatians 5:1 and stand fast in this freedom by which Christ has made me free.

Just because we have revelation concerning an issue does not mean we cannot backslide in it. That is why I keep myself stirred up about walking in love. I enjoy preaching and teaching on the subject. I like to read about it, talk to others about it and, above all else, put it into practice in my daily life.

I pray that you will make it a daily part of your life too.

DO YOU FEEL LIKE A SLAVE?

So if the Son liberates you [makes you free men], then
you are really and unquestionably free.

—JOHN 8:36

Many people feel like slaves in their own homes, or slaves on their job. Perhaps there are those who are taking advantage of them, but a wrong mental attitude can also be the problem.

I have discovered that some believers are willing to do things for others at church and see it as part of their ministry, and yet are unwilling to do the same things at home for their family members without feeling like a slave.

Some people may be perfectly willing to make a fruit salad for their church leaders as a ministry, but feel that they are being taken advantage of if they are called upon to do the same thing for a family member. Or they may be more than happy to pick up sister so and so and give her a ride to church, but feel put out if their own mother asks them to take her to the bank.

I know this is true because I went through all those phases and learned all about such things as God was dealing with me about them in my own life. I didn't get these messages out of a five-dollar sermon book. I have lived them, and I know what works and what doesn't work. Selfishness does not work, but love does.

In Mark 5 we read about a man who was so demon-possessed that Jesus cast a legion of demons out of him. (v. 15.) Being set free, the man then wanted to follow Jesus wherever He went. He begged Jesus to take him with Him, but Jesus told the man, . . . *Go home to your own [family and relatives and friends] and bring back word to them of how much the Lord has done for you . . .* (v. 19).

When the Lord has done something wonderful for us, like saving us or healing us or setting us free from some kind of bondage, often we get all excited and want to be with Him constantly. We want to spend all of our time in Bible studies and prayer groups or doing church work. Often, we forget to go home and show our friends and relatives how much He has done for us.

Let the people in your sphere of influence see the changes in you. It will do more toward winning them than anything you could ever say, especially if you give them words with no action.

DO YOU FEEL LIKE A MARTYR?

> *I beseech you therefore, brethren, by the mercies of God, that you present your bodies a living sacrifice, holy, acceptable to God, which is your reasonable service.*
> —ROMANS 12:1 NKJV

A martyr is a great and constant sufferer, and in some instances, one who lets everyone know he is suffering.

I absolutely despise for people to do something for me and then by their words or attitude let me know they are doing it, but they really don't want to. If someone is going to bless me, then I want that person to do it with a smile.

According to Romans 12:1, God is looking for living sacrifices, not martyrs.

I once knew a woman who felt like a slave to her family and definitely had the attitude of a martyr. I got very tired of hearing her continually talk about how much she did for everyone and how little anyone appreciated her. I could tell she kept a running account of what she was doing for "them" versus what "they" were doing for her. Eventually she was successful in ruining her marriage and most of her relationships with her children.

True martyrs don't know they are martyrs. They gladly suffer personally to do the will of God. They do it without calling attention to it or even giving any thought to it. They are totally unconcerned about themselves and their sacrifices for the sake of others. False martyrs, on the other hand, think of nothing else but themselves and their "sacrifices."

Our biggest problem is we ask ourselves far too often how we *feel* about things.

Someone recently asked me how I liked all the traveling we must do in connection with our ministry. At that time I was gone from home approximately 60 percent of the time. I was amazed when I tried to answer that question. I realized I had not asked myself in a long, long time how I liked traveling to do ministry; I had simply made up my mind to do it.

We need to discover what God wants us to do and just do it. We don't need to make a big deal out of all our sacrifices.

All those who fulfill the call of God on their lives must sacrifice in some way in order to do it, and often their families must sacrifice to support their call.

My children had to sacrifice having what the world would call a "normal mother." My husband certainly has not had a "normal wife." As a matter of fact, not much about our lives has been normal or status quo. But we have all made it through the hard times, and now we are all reaping the benefits of not giving up when things were difficult.

I was a good wife and mother, even though perhaps not a normal one by the world's standards. But regardless of what I had to sacrifice to answer the call on my life, I never felt like a martyr, and neither should you.

Be a servant, not a martyr!

BEING A SERVANT REQUIRES WASHING FEET

[Now] before the Passover Feast began, Jesus knew (was fully aware) that the time had come for Him to leave this world and return to the Father. And as He had loved those who were His own in the world, He loved them to the last and to the highest degree.

Jesus . . . Got up from supper, took off His garments, and taking a [servant's] towel, He fastened it around His waist.

Then He poured water into the washbasin and began to wash the disciples' feet and to wipe them with the [servant's] towel with which He was girded.

—John 13:1,3,4,5

In John 13 we see the premier example of servanthood as Jesus took off His garments, put on a servant's towel and began to wash the disciples' feet.

In those days men wore sandals, and the roads were not paved. As a matter of fact, they were not even covered with gravel; they were plain old dirt. By the time the day ended, the disciples' feet were really dirty, and Jesus offered to wash them. He chose this rather menial task to teach His disciples a great lesson, saying, . . . *Unless I wash you, you have no part with (in) Me [you have no share in companionship with Me]* (v. 8).

Then in verses 13 through 17 He went on to explain clearly the meaning of what He had just done:

> *You call Me the Teacher (Master) and the Lord, and you are right in doing so, for that is what I am.*
>
> *If I then, your Lord and Teacher (Master), have washed your feet, you ought [it is your duty, you are under obligation, you owe it] to wash one another's feet.*
>
> *For I have given you this as an example, so that you should do [in your turn] what I have done to you.*
>
> *I assure you, most solemnly I tell you, A servant is not greater than his master, and no one who is sent is superior to the one who sent him.*
>
> *If you know these things, blessed and happy and to be envied are you if you practice them [if you act accordingly and really do them].*

What I learned from this passage is that we must do things for each other; otherwise, we are really not part of one another. The things we do to serve one another is what bonds our relationships together.

My brother and only sibling lived in sin for a good part of his life, but in 1998 he gave his life to Jesus and for many months after that, he lived with us in our home. Since no one had ever done very much for him, he had no idea what real love was. So we have had to show him the love of Jesus.

Our family does a lot of nice things for him. I often buy him clothes, because I know he really likes to dress sharp. He rubs my back and neck almost every night, because he knows that is something that I really enjoy. By the time I have sat at my computer working on a book for nine or ten hours, I need a good back massage.

My brother and I are very close; actually my entire family is very close to him. I believe our relationship was not bonded together by blood alone, but by serving one another.

What my brother and I do for one another is the equivalent of washing each other's feet. By being a servant to one another, we show our love for each other, which is what Jesus told us to do in John 13.

ARE YOU FREE TO SERVE?

He who is greatest among you shall be your servant.

Whoever exalts himself [with haughtiness and empty pride] shall be humbled (brought low), and whoever humbles himself [whoever has a modest

*opinion of himself and behaves accordingly] shall be
raised to honor.*

—MATTHEW 23:11,12

Jesus was able to wash His disciples' feet because He was free. Only a person who is truly free, one who is not insecure, can do menial tasks and not feel insignificant as a result.

So much of our worth and value is connected to what we do that it makes it very difficult for us to enjoy serving. Serving others is not viewed as a high position, and yet Jesus said it is the highest of all.

Serving others also sets them free to love. It disarms even the most hateful individual. It is actually fun to watch that person's amazement when he realizes he is being served through love.

If someone knows full well he has done us wrong, and we return his evil with good, it begins to tear down the walls he has built around himself. Sooner or later he will begin to trust us and start learning from us what real love is.

That is the whole purpose behind being a servant, to show others the love of God that He has shown us so that they too can share in it — and then pass it on.

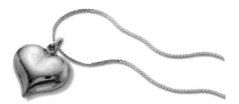

13

LOVE IS LIBERATING

*Now the Lord is the Spirit, and where the Spirit of
the Lord is, there is liberty (emancipation from bondage, freedom).*

—2 CORINTHIANS 3:17

Love offers people both roots and wings. It provides a sense of
belonging (roots) and a sense of freedom (wings). Love does not
try to control or manipulate others. It does not try to reach fulfillment through the destiny of others.

How many parents push their children to do things they do not
even want to do just to meet the frustrated desires of the parents?

A father wanted to be a professional basketball player, but he
missed out on the opportunity, so now he pushes his son to be
what he himself wanted to be. But the son has less athletic ability
than his father and no real desire to excel in sports of any kind.

A mother wants her daughter to be popular because she herself
never was. She pushes her daughter to be a cheerleader, to join

social clubs at school and to participate in numerous extracurricular activities. She manipulates circumstances so that her daughter will be with all the "right" people. The daughter may want nothing to do with any of it. She may be the quiet, retiring type who prefers to remain in the background.

Many women push their husbands to climb the ladder of success in business or make progress in politics. Many husbands pressure their wives to be something or do something that does not even remotely interest them.

That is not the way true love works. It does not try to gain personal satisfaction at the expense of others.

If you and I really love something, we must take a chance on setting it free. If it really belongs to us, it will come back to us.

A caged bird cannot fly!

Release the people in your life to be all they can be for God's glory, not your own.

PROCLAIM LIBERTY

> *The Spirit of the Lord God is upon me, because the Lord has anointed and qualified me to preach the Gospel of good tidings to the meek, the poor, and afflicted; He has sent me to bind up and heal the brokenhearted, to proclaim liberty to the [physical and spiritual] captives. . . .*
>
> —ISAIAH 61:1

Jesus said that He was sent by God to proclaim liberty. As believers, that is what we are meant to do also — to free people to fulfill God's will for their lives, not to bring them under our control.

Paul said he was free from anyone's control, but he made himself a bond slave to all for Christ's sake (in order to win them to Him). (1 Corinthians 9:19.)

I have discovered that trying to make people do what I want them to do closes the door for God to speak to their heart. What I am trying to get them to do may be something they would do anyway, but everyone wants to make their own choices.

Proclaim liberty. Set people free and see what they do.

THE GIFT OF FREEDOM

And you recently turned around and repented, doing what was right in My sight by proclaiming liberty each one to his neighbor. . . .

—JEREMIAH 34:15

For years I tried desperately to remold my husband and children until I finally realized it was an act of selfishness, not love. I told myself that I simply wanted God's best for them; however, I had decided what His best was and was trying to force it upon them.

Proverbs 22:6 tells us that we are to train up our children in the way they should go, and when they are old, they will not depart from it. Ephesians 6:4 tells us that we are not to irritate and provoke our children, not to exasperate them to resentment, but to bring them up tenderly and in the training, discipline, counsel and admonition of the Lord. Scriptures such as these shed light on the proper attitude we as parents should have toward our children.

To be honest, that was not the way I brought up my children. I wanted all of them to preach, and pressured them to go in that direction, but it does not look like that will happen.

Actually, I now realize that really wasn't even what would have blessed me after all. Each of them fulfills a different function in the ministry that is very needful for me, and I would really be missing something if I had gotten my way with them. Two of them have speaking gifts — one wants nothing to do with talking in front of people, and one hasn't made his mind up yet. God is in control, and I am glad. Trying to control others is hard work.

Give the gift of freedom. People will love you for it. Obviously this does not mean letting your children or employees do whatever they want to do. But it does mean learning the balance between your being in control and God's being in control.

The Greek translation of *liberty* in the Bible is defined as "a loosening, relaxation."[1] Make sure the atmosphere in your home and business is a relaxed one, not one that makes people feel if they don't please you all the time tension will fill the air and tempers will explode.

Relax. Loosen up a bit. Give the gift of freedom.

OVERCOME FEAR WITH LOVE

> *Let no one then seek his own good and advantage and profit, but [rather] each one of the other [let him seek the welfare of his neighbor].*
>
> —1 CORINTHIANS 10:24

Fear restrains most of us. We are afraid we will never get what we want in life if we don't try to make it happen ourselves. We should never try to derive our identity from another person, nor should we impose ours upon anyone else.

Know who you are, be free to reach your full potential, but learn to operate in trust with God and with others, not in fear. Don't be afraid that if you don't make your dreams come true, you will lose out in life.

Neither you nor I should try to control the destiny of another human being. It is not our right, and God will not permit it. Try to influence others in a positive way. Help them be all they can be, but don't cross the line and take away their liberty.

Fear is the emotion that influences us most in life, but that can be changed. What are we afraid of? Being needy or alone, suffering pain or loss? We try to manipulate people to be sure they are always in our lives. We want to keep them dependent upon us, so we never have to depend on them.

Some parents try so hard to keep their children under their wings, they end up losing them.

Our family is together most of the time, but we all have freedom. We are very involved in each other's lives, but we don't try to control one another.

Whatever God gives us, we must learn to hold loosely in our hands. If we don't own anything, we cannot lose anything. We are stewards over our children, not masters and owners. They really belong to God, and He has endowed them with the right of free choice. We must learn to love people — not try to own them or make them over into our image.

A person who has great love is one who is able to release people and things. He does so because he has himself been released by the love of God.

I so much appreciate the freedom that Jesus has given me; I want everyone to experience the joy of knowing it.

CONCLUSION

And so faith, hope, love abide [faith – conviction and
belief respecting man's relation to God and divine
things; hope – joyful and confident expectation of
eternal salvation; love – true affection for God and
man, growing out of God's love for and in us], these
three; but the greatest of these is love.

—1 CORINTHIANS 13:13

As we have seen, love is the greatest thing in life, and walking in love should be our main focus. *God is love,* and He wants us to love one another (1 John 4:11,16). We can only truly love others by receiving and expressing His love. In order to do that, we need to understand that He loves us, and accept His love. When we do, we begin a love walk that causes us to live in a new way — a new way of thinking, a new way of speaking and a new way of acting.

Love can be expressed in many different ways, but one factor is always the same — love gives. *Vine's Complete Expository Dictionary of Old and New Testament Words* states: "Love can be known only from the actions it prompts. God's love is seen in the gift of His Son (1 John 4:9,10). But obviously this is not the love of complacency, or affection. . . . It was an exercise of the divine will in deliberate choice, made without assignable cause save that which lies in the nature of God Himself (Deuteronomy 7:7,8). . . .

"Christian love, whether exercised toward the brethren, or toward men generally, is not an impulse from the feelings, it does not always run with the natural inclinations, nor does it spend itself only upon those for whom some affinity is discovered. Love seeks the welfare of all (Romans 15:2), and works no ill to any, (vs. 13:8-10); love seeks opportunity to do good to 'all men . . .' (Galatians 6:10)."[1]

Walking in love is not a natural lifestyle for people (especially when they are going through personal trials). It takes effort, involvement and sacrifice. But believers are equipped with the power of the Holy Spirit to make it possible for them to walk in love at all times.

In this book, I have shared some of the things the Lord has taught me about love over the years, but I have certainly not exhausted all the ways there are to walk in love. I still have much to learn about it, and I hope I learn so much that someday I can write a sequel to this book.

We have seen that we love by the words we speak, by sharing our material goods, and even by our thoughts.

We have also seen that love has many facets. Love is patient and enduring. It is not envious or jealous, proud, boastful or rude. Love forgives; it is not easily offended. Love is unconditional; it always believes the best about others. It is liberating because it sets us free from "self." Love is actually a form of spiritual warfare. We must never lose our burning desire to practice it every day because by walking in love, we become overcomers in life.

I pray that you will get addicted to walking in love and blessing people. Give Satan a nervous breakdown — become uncontrollable in your love walk by joining me in praying, *Lord, reduce me to love!*

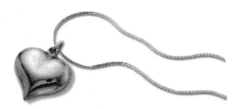

Prayer for a Personal Relationship with the Lord

God wants you to receive His free gift of salvation. Jesus wants to save you and fill you with the Holy Spirit more than anything. If you have never invited Jesus, the Prince of Peace, to be your Lord and Savior, I invite you to do so now. Pray the following prayer, and if you are really sincere about it, you will experience a new life in Christ.

Father,

You loved the world so much, You gave Your only begotten Son to die for our sins so that whoever believes in Him will not perish, but have eternal life.

Your Word says we are saved by grace through faith as a gift from You. There is nothing we can do to earn salvation.

I believe and confess with my mouth that Jesus Christ is Your Son, the Savior of the world. I believe He died on the cross for me and bore all of my sins, paying the price for them. I believe in my heart that You raised Jesus from the dead.

I ask You to forgive my sins. I confess Jesus as my Lord. According to Your Word, I am saved and will spend eternity with You! Thank You, Father. I am so grateful! In Jesus' name, amen.

See John 3:16; Ephesians 2:8,9; Romans 10:9,10; 1 Corinthians 15:3,4; 1 John 1:9; 4:14-16; 5:1,12,13.

ENDNOTES

Introduction

[1] *Webster's II New College Dictionary* (Boston/New York: Houghton Mifflin Company, 1995), s.v. "reduce."

Chapter 1

[1] *Webster's II,* s.v. "trademark."

[2] *Webster's New World™ College Dictionary, Fourth Edition,* (New York: Macmillan USA, 1999), s.v. "thirsty."

[3] *Webster's II,* s.v. "pursue."

[4] *Webster's II,* s.v. "seek."

[5] Henry Drummond, *The Greatest Thing in the World* (London: Hodder and Stoughton, 1980), p. 42.

Chapter 4

[1] *Webster's II,* s.v. "mercy."

Chapter 6

[1] *American Dictionary of the English Language,* 10th Ed. (San Francisco: Foundation for American Christian Education, 1998).

Facsimile of Noah Webster's 1828 edition, permission to reprint by G. & C. Merriam Company, copyright 1967 & 1995 (Renewal) by Rosalie J. Slater, s.v. "RESPECT."

[2] *Webster's New World™ College Dictionary, Third Edition*, (New York: Macmillan USA, 1999 by Simon & Schuster, Inc.), s.v. "preference."

Chapter 7

[1] Debra Baker, "Beyond Ozzie and Harriet," *ABA Journal*, (Chicago: Copyright American Bar Association, September 1998).

[2] William A. Galston, "Divorce American Style," *Public Interest*, No. 124, Summer 1996, p. 14.

Chapter 10

[1] Creflo A. Dollar Jr., *The Color of Love: Understanding God's Answer to Racism, Separation and Division* (Tulsa: Harrison House, 1997).

[2] Shirley Terry, "Mrs. Anderson's Roses," *Guideposts*, (May, 1999), pp. 10-12.

[3] *MATTHEW HENRY'S COMMENTARY ON THE WHOLE BIBLE: New Modern Edition, Electronic Database*. Copyright 1991 by Hendrickson Publishers, Inc. Matthew 15:21-28, "The Canaanite's daughter healed." Used by permission. All rights reserved.

[4] *ENCYCLOPAEDIA JUDAICA*, Volume 16, UR-Z, Supplementary Entries,(Jerusalem, Israel: Keterpress Enterprises, 1978), **WOMAN. Legal Status and Religious Participation.** pp. 624-625.

Chapter 11

[1] *Webster's 1828 Edition*, s.v. "holiness."

[2] W. E. Vine, *Vine's Complete Expository Dictionary of Old and New Testament Words* (Nashville: Thomas Nelson Inc., 1984), "An

Expository Dictionary of New Testament Words," p. 233, s.v. "FERVENT, FERVENTLY," C. **Verb,** *zeo.*

Chapter 13

[1] Vine, p. 366, s.v. "LIBERTY," **A. Nouns,** No. 1 *anesis.*

Conclusion

[1] Vine, "New Testament Words," pp. 381-382, s.v. "LOVE," **A. Verbs,** No. 1. *agapao.*

ABOUT THE AUTHOR

Joyce Meyer has been teaching the Word of God since 1976 and in full-time ministry since 1980. She is the bestselling author of more than fifty inspirational books, including *How to Hear from God, Knowing God Intimately,* and *Battlefield of the Mind.* She has also released thousands of teaching cassettes and a complete video library. Joyce's *Enjoying Everyday Life* radio and television programs are broadcast around the world, and she travels extensively conducting conferences. Joyce and her husband Dave are the parents of four grown children and make their home in St. Louis, Missouri.

To contact the author write:

Joyce Meyer Ministries
P. O. Box 655
Fenton, Missouri 63026
or call: (636) 349-0303
Internet Address: www.joycemeyer.org

Please include your testimony or help received from this book when you write. Your prayer requests are welcome.

To contact the author
in Canada, please write:
Joyce Meyer Ministries Canada, Inc.
Lambeth Box 1300
London, ON N6P 1T5
or call: (636) 349-0303

In Australia, please write:
Joyce Meyer Ministries-Australia
Locked Bag 77
Mansfield Delivery Centre
Queensland 4122
or call: 07 3349 1200

In England, please write:
Joyce Meyer Ministries
P. O. Box 1549
Windsor
SL4 1GT
Or call: (0) 1753-831102

BOOKS BY JOYCE MEYER

STARTING YOUR DAY RIGHT

BEAUTY FOR ASHES REVISED EDITION

HOW TO HEAR FROM GOD

KNOWING GOD INTIMATELY

THE POWER OF FORGIVENESS

THE POWER OF DETERMINATION

THE POWER OF BEING POSITIVE

THE SECRETS OF SPIRITUAL POWER

THE BATTLE BELONGS TO THE LORD

SECRETS TO EXCEPTIONAL LIVING

EIGHT WAYS TO KEEP THE DEVIL UNDER YOUR FEET

TEENAGERS ARE PEOPLE TOO!

FILLED WITH THE SPIRIT

CELEBRATION OF SIMPLICITY

THE JOY OF BELIEVING PRAYER

NEVER LOSE HEART

BEING THE PERSON GOD MADE YOU TO BE

A LEADER IN THE MAKING

"GOOD MORNING, THIS IS GOD!" GIFT BOOK

JESUS—NAME ABOVE ALL NAMES

"GOOD MORNING, THIS IS GOD!" DAILY CALENDAR

HELP ME—I'M MARRIED!

REDUCE ME TO LOVE

BE HEALED IN JESUS' NAME

HOW TO SUCCEED AT BEING YOURSELF

EAT AND STAY THIN

WEARY WARRIORS, FAINTING SAINTS

LIFE IN THE WORD JOURNAL

LIFE IN THE WORD DEVOTIONAL

BE ANXIOUS FOR NOTHING
BE ANXIOUS FOR NOTHING STUDY GUIDE
STRAIGHT TALK ON LONELINESS
STRAIGHT TALK ON FEAR
STRAIGHT TALK ON INSECURITY
STRAIGHT TALK ON DISCOURAGEMENT
STRAIGHT TALK ON WORRY
STRAIGHT TALK ON DEPRESSION
STRAIGHT TALK ON STRESS
DON'T DREAD
MANAGING YOUR EMOTIONS
HEALING THE BROKENHEARTED
ME AND MY BIG MOUTH!
ME AND MY BIG MOUTH! STUDY GUIDE
PREPARE TO PROSPER
DO IT AFRAID!
EXPECT A MOVE OF GOD IN YOUR LIFE . . .
SUDDENLY!
ENJOYING WHERE YOU ARE ON THE WAY TO
WHERE YOU ARE GOING
THE MOST IMPORTANT DECISION YOU WILL EVER
MAKE
WHEN, GOD, WHEN?
WHY, GOD, WHY?
THE WORD, THE NAME, THE BLOOD
BATTLEFIELD OF THE MIND
BATTLEFIELD OF THE MIND STUDY GUIDE
TELL THEM I LOVE THEM
PEACE
THE ROOT OF REJECTION

BEAUTY FOR ASHES
IF NOT FOR THE GRACE OF GOD
IF NOT FOR THE GRACE OF GOD STUDY GUIDE